MIRACLES

FROM

GOD OR MAN?

BY

JIMMY JIVIDEN

Gospel Advocate Company
Nashville, Tennessee

© 2005 Gospel Advocate Co.

Second Edition. Reprinted

First Edition, 1987.

Published by Gospel Advocate Co.
1006 Elm Hill Pike, Nashville, TN 37210
http://www.gospeladvocate.com

ISBN: 0-89225-544-7

DEDICATION

to Shirley

TABLE OF CONTENTS

MIRACLES FROM GOD OR MAN?

JIMMY JIVIDEN

PREFACE

Should we "Expect A Miracle" for our lives today as suggested by the title of a popular television program? Should we trust those who claim the power to perform miracles and give our hopes and our money to them?

Jimmy Jividen's excellent research into this subject provides a benificial service to all who will read and study the materials he has amassed. He clears the air greatly by providing lucid definitions of important terminology related to the study of miracles. He presents a thorough study of miracles in th New Teseament and he sets forth plainly the purpose of Biblical miracles.

The study includes a contrast between New Testament miracles and miracles claimed by the first century pagan world. He then examines the alleged miracles of today and presents strong reasons to question contemporary claims of miraculous power.

Millions are confused about claims of miraculous powers and cures. Thousands are injured physically because they are led by false hopes to faith healers who may temporarily help the psychological problems, but often tragically and fatally delay the person getting genuine help for his real physical problems. Multiplied thousands of people are disillusioned and reject Christianity altogether when their hopes are dashed and they realize that the claim to miraculous power is false. Unbelievers are aided in their attempts to destroy faith when they are able to expose fake healers and declare that much of Christianity is filled with superstition and irrational concepts.

Armed with the information provided in this work by Jimmy Jividen, one can help sincere, misled beleivers in Christ to an accurate and biblical understanding of miracles. One can also overcome the arguments of unbelievers who try to destroy faith in biblical miracles.

Jividen's scholarly and thorough study of miracles is vitally needed. It should be read and used by every concerned Christian because it will place in their hands and minds important imformation essential to dealing with one of the major issues in today's relegious circles.

F. Furman Kearley, Ph.D.
Editor, *Gospel Advocate*

ACKNOWLEDGEMENTS

I am indebted to a multitude of people for the material I have presented in this book. Many of the authors from whom I have learned are in the footnotes. Much of my understanding of God's work in both the natural and the supernatural realms has come from my study in response to questions and suggestions I received at lectures I have presented on Glossolalia and the Holy Spirit.

To those who read the manuscript I owe a special debt of gratitude for correcting errors, offering suggestions and sharpening my focus. Everett Ferguson, Phil and Boots Nichols, Furman Kearley and Clark Potts all contributed to the final form. James Fulbright and the ACU Press have been especially helpful in finishing the final stages of the book.

My family, and especially my wife Shirley, has been my helper and enabler for the task.

CHAPTER 1

DEFINITIONS

The word, miracle, is an elusive term. It means different things to different people. It has different meanings in different contexts.

It is sometimes used to refer to that which is awesome. One would understand this meaning if he heard someone say, "The miracle of new life at springtime..." or "The miracle of new life when a child is born..." or "The miracle of a changed life when one becomes a Christian..."

It is sometimes used to refer to that which is out of the ordinary, or that which is not expected. One would understand this meaning if he heard someone say, "It is a miracle that he was not injured in the automobile accident..." or "It is a miracle that the cinderella team won the tournament..." or "It is a miracle that he recovered from cancer...".

It is sometimes used to refer to that which is believed to be providential. One would understand this meaning if he heard someone say, "Our business success was a miracle..." or "It was a miracle that we raised the funds we needed to send out another missionary..." or "It was a miracle that he got well...".

There is nothing technically wrong with the use of the term "miracle" in these ways. The meaning of words is determined by their usage. The same word can mean radically different things in different contexts. The term "football" means one kind of game to an American sports fan and an entirely different game to the European sports fan.

Often the contemporary confusion about miracles comes from confusing the popular use of the word with the meaning reflected in the

New Testament. There are unique qualities involved in the New Testament miracles which must not be confused with the popular use of the term.

There is in the teachings of Confucius a doctrine called the "Rectification of Names". He expresses the importance of calling things by terms that all will understand.

> *If the designations are not accurate, language will not*
> *be clear. If language is not clear, duties will not be*
> *carried out. If duties are not carried out, rites and music*
> *will not flourish. If rites and music do not flourish, then*
> *punishments will not be specific. If punishments are*
> *not specific, then people will do nothing without getting*
> *into trouble.[1]*

Much of the trouble and confusion about miracles is caused by the looseness in which the term "miracle" is used. Alice in Wonderland might be able to give whatever meaning she wanted to any term, but such a policy will not aid understanding the teachings of the Scriptures about miracles.

New Testament Terms

To understand what is involved in New Testament miracles, one should begin by examining the root meaning of the terms which were used to describe them. There are four --- signs, wonders, miracles and works. Each word has shades of meaning which add different dimensions to our understanding.

Two passages list three of these words together. Perhaps this indicates that no one word is big enough to express the full meaning of the miraculous event.

One of the proofs that Peter used to convince the multitude on the Day of Pentecost that Jesus was the Christ was the miracles which Jesus worked in his personal ministry.

> *. . .Jesus the Nazarene, a man attested to you by*
> *God with miracles and wonders and signs which God*
> *performed through Him in your midst. . . [2]*

2

Notice the three dimensions of the miracles of Jesus. There were signs, wonders and miracles. Notice also the purpose was "to attest" that Jesus was approved of God.

In warning the Hebrews of neglecting their salvation, a similar passage is found. The author says that the message of salvation which had first been spoken by the Lord was confirmed with miracles.

> . . .*God also bearing witness with them both by signs*
> *and and wonders and by varous miracles and by gifts*
> *of the Holy Spirit according to His own will. . .*[3]

Notice that these three words are again used together along with the gifts of the Holy Spirit. Notice the purpose was to bear witness to Jesus and His message.

The word translated "sign" is *semeion*. Its meaning, like the English word "sign" points to something beyond itself. A street sign is not the street, but points beyond itself to the street it identifies. The miraculous events of the New Testament are not to be seen as events centering on themselves. They are to be seen as pointing to Jesus, His apostles and others to show that God approved of the man and his message. The word "sign" focuses on the purpose of the miraculous event.

The word translated "wonder" is *teras*. Its meaning, like the English word "wonder", refers to the viewer's response of awe or terror upon witnessing an event. The word reflects the kind of feeling one would have in viewing the Northern Lights in the Alaskan sky, seeing the Grand Canyon at sundown or a father witnessing the birth of his child. An illustration of this feeling can be seen in the response of Peter, James and John on the mount of Transfiguration. When they saw Moses and Elijah and heard the voice of God, Matthew records:

> . . .*And when the disciples heard this, they fell on*
> *their faces and were much afraid. . .*[4]

The focus of this word is the viewer's response to a miraculous event.

Luke emphasizes this aspect of the miracles.[5] The people who witnessed the miracles were "amazed", "astonished" and "filled with fear". One of the words used to describe the response of the people was *ekstasis*.[6] This word comes from the preposition, "*ek*" and the verb, "*isthimi*". It means "to stand outside of oneself". It is the root for the English word "ecstasy". The people responded to Jesus' miracles in awe and wonder.

> *And they were all seized with astonishment and began
> glorifying God; and they were filled with fear saying, We have
> seen remarkable things today.*[7]

The word translated "miracle" is *dunamis*. The meaning is power. The English words "dynamite" and "dynamo" come from this word. The word reflects the power source of the miraculous event. Miraculous events in the New Testament do not just happen. They have to be caused by power. It must be power that can suspend the laws of nature. It must be superhuman power. It was a recognition of this kind of power that caused Nicodemus to say to Jesus:

> *. . .No one can do these signs that You do unless
> God is with Him. . .*[8]

The possessing of power --- superhuman power --- was a prerequisite to performing a miracle. The apostles received power when they were sent out by Jesus[9] and when the Holy Spirit came upon them on the Day of Pentecost.[10] It was this kind of power that was sought by Simon the Sorcerer.[11] The focus of this word is the power source by which miracles were performed.

The fourth word used for the miraculous event in the New Testament is *ergon*. It is translated "work". This word is extensively used in John for the miraculous works done by Jesus and which he identifies as coming from the Father.[12] The context in which it is generally used refers to the works done by Jesus as being a basis for men to believe on Him.

> *. . .If I do not do the works of My father, do not believe
> Me; but if I do them, though you do not believe Me,
> believe the works. . .*[13]

The focus of the word is the event itself --- the actual miraculous event.

The use of these four terms reflect different aspects of the miracles of the New Testament. They came from supernatural power. They struck awe and wonder in the hearts of those who witnessed them. They pointed, not to themselves, but to the man who worked them or the message he spoke. They were confirming signs. They are identified as works of the Father which were designed to produce faith.

It should be noted, however, that all of these Greek terms are neutral. They do not, in the meaning of the word itself, carry the idea of being contrary to the natural laws of the universe. All of these terms are used in other passages completely outside of the miraculous context.

One must go beyond the meaning of the terms themselves to understand the New Testament miracles. This can be done by looking at the events within the context in which they appear. What is it that makes the miraculous events of the New Testament unique?

Three Kinds of Events

The New Testament miracles are unique because they are contrary to or above the normal observable patterns of the universe. To walk on water, to cure a man born blind, to make a forty year old cripple leap and to resurrect a man who had been dead three days are not normal happenings. It is the fact that they are not normal happenings that makes them unique and allows them to fulfill their designated purpose of confirmation.

One can classify the events which have happened in the world into three categories. This classification will illustrate the uniqueness of the New Testament miracles.

First, there are miracles. They are of supernatural origin. They are different from, above or contrary to the natural order of things as we know them in the world. New Testament miracles fit this category.

Second, there is the normal. This is what we are able to observe by our senses and reason from our mind. The normal is so static that it is the basis for the development of the scientific method. Sometimes this normal is called the laws of nature. These laws were spoken into existence at the creation of the world. They follow a pattern --- like a seed bringing forth after its kind. The normal is orderly, consistent and predictable. We are able to understand the cause and effect. An example of this is that an acorn will grow into an oak tree. It is expected because the same thing has happened in the same way multitude millions of times.

Third, there is the paranormal. This means "along side" of the normal. This is not miraculous because there is nothing in this event which would contradict the laws of nature as we know them. It is not normal because the event is different from the usual. One is unable to understand its cause and effect. Many things which fall into this category may be understood at some later time. Their cause and effect may become evident when a greater knowledge of the universe and the circumstances which surrounded the event are known.

One might not understand what makes a forked stick turn down when a person "witches water". It sometimes does for some people. Someday someone will probably understand why. For now one can only say that such is not contrary to any laws of nature as we know them, but neither do we understand the causes. That makes it paranormal.

Hypnosis is another phenomenon which can be classed as paranormal. One does not understand all of the causes and effects associated with it. Some individuals are more easily hypnotized than others. One might not know why. Hypnotism does not contradict any of the laws of nature that are known. It does not fit known normal causes. It is paranormal.

Attempts to Explain Miracles

In attempting to explain the miracles of the New Testament, categories similar to those mentioned above have been used.

Some would understand New Testament miracles as being nothing more than normal happenings misunderstood by primitive and ignorant men. According to them, Jesus did not really walk on water. He just appeared to do so because of the vantage point from which the apostles viewed Him from the shoreline. The five thousand were not really fed by the miracle of the loaves and fishes, but by the amazing generosity which prompted the multitude to share their lunch with one another.

Spinoza, the seventeeneth-century Jewish philosopher, under-

stood miracles as being either the figment of an uneducated imagination
or events that could not be explained in a primitive time.[14]

William Barclay, in discussing the miracle of changing the
water into wine, questions the reality of the event being supernatural.
He writes:

> . . .*I am certain that again and again Jesus was taking natural
> events and in them was discovering God and showing God to
> men.[15]*

To him it would appear, miracles were mere natural events through
which men are able to see God. Such miracles, he says, still happen if
only we have eyes to see and a mind to understand.

English Deists in the seventeeneth century perceived the world
as being a closed system. The God of Creation wound the world up
like a clock and is letting it run down without intervention. If such
were the case, then the New Testament miracles could not have
happened in the way that they were recorded in the Scriptures.[16] A multitude of authors, like Barclay, have accepted these conclusions but
wish to retain the "spiritual significance" of the miracles. The results
end up being a contradiction. One cannot hold on to the spiritual values
of Jesus' teachings and at the same time deny the miraculous events
which confirmed them. One cannot acknowledge the Divinity of Jesus
and at the same time deny those events which bore witness to this Divinity.

Neo Orthodoxy with its existential presuppositions has sought
to give religious respectability to the denial of the New Testament miracles. Writers with such presuppositions use Christian terminology but
with new meanings. While denying absolute, objective, universal
truth, they seek to hold on to an individually perceived subjective truth.
An event is a miracle, according to their teachings, not because it is real
or true. It is a miracle because it is perceived as being so by the one
who witnessed it. The problem with such a schizophrenic faith is that it
is no faith at all. It is no more than the shell of traditional cultural
values which one desires to hold on to, but one cannot because he no
longer believes in that which validates their authority. The fantasy of a
fake faith cannot resolve this contradiction. One cannot separate the person of Jesus from either His teachings or His miracles. One demands

the other. The passing of time shows that a religious institution cannot long endure after it begins to doubt the contents of its faith. The pages of history are filled with tombstones of dead religious movements which apostatized, digressed, divided or died because they compromised the content of their faith.

When a person begins to doubt the credibility of the Scriptures in regard to its miracles, it will only be a matter of time until he doubts both its teachings and the Christ to which they bear witness. It is true that such men may hide their doubts with hypocrisy, the smoke screen of theological language or mere silence, but their lives and the lives of those people whom they influence will ultimately reveal it. If one questions the miracles of the New Testament as being real, how can such a one accept the message to which they bear witness?

Some would understand the New Testament miracles as being paranormal events. That is, they are within the realm of the laws of nature, but they are beyond the knowledge of the men who witnessed them. They were not contrary to the observable laws of the universe that were understood, but men were unable to understand the cause and effect which produced the event.

Many of the healing miracles of Jesus would be put in this category. Jesus could cure leprosy, heal the blind, cure the cripples and raise those who were dead because He was far beyond His time in understanding illness and its cures. What He did was heal according to natural laws, but since the people of His day did not understand His methods, people perceived His healing as miraculous.

One as prominent as Augustine seemed to lean toward this view. He suggests that miracles are not contrary to nature -- only contrary to nature so far as known by man.[17]

It would also appear that C. S. Lewis would be close to this view. It is true that he understands a miracle to mean, "An interference with Nature by supernatural power"[18], but then later says:

> . . .*A miracle is emphatically not an event without cause or without results. Its cause is the activity of God; Its results follow according to Natural law. . .*[19]

The way that he comes to this conclusion is by posing the possibility of there being other systems in addition to the system one calls nature.

8

> . . .*The Supernaturalist believes that one Thing exists on*
> *its own and has produced the framework of space and time and*
> *the procession of systematically connected events which*
> *fill them. This framework, and this filling, he calls Nature.*
> *It may, or may not, be the only reality which the one Primary*
> *Thing has produced. There might be other systems in addition*
> *to the one we call Nature. . .*[20]

He is suggesting that the system of reality we call Nature might be touched with another system of reality because of a supernatural power and that this contact would change Nature as we know it. This, he suggests, would be a miracle.

Such an explanation would be paranormal from the vantage point of the supernatural power who controls the different Natures. The point at which another system of reality would touch Nature would be considered a miracle to those within the system because nothing like that had ever happened before. Even though it is abnormal in our system, it would be normal in the many possible systems of the supernatural power.

Lewis' writings on miracles have perhaps been one of the most influential of our time. Certainly it deals with the issues involved. The following points perhaps need to be considered before accepting his conclusions.

First, Lewis' purpose is to show the philosophical reasonableness of miracles much as Plato and Aristotle showed the philosophical reasonableness of the first cause by arguing for the Form of the Good and the Unmoved Mover. By this approach Lewis has shown that the position of the supernaturalist is as reasonable as the position of the naturalist. One learns much from such a study, but one must not let this be confused with the Biblical theology on miracles.

Second, Lewis has indeed developed a theory to explain how an orderly God can consistently alter that orderliness of nature with a miracle which is inconsistent with all events before. This he has done by going beyond the realm of Nature as men know it to another system of a different dimension. That which seems inconsistent in the realm of Nature as it is known by man may be very consistent in another realm. This does not solve the problem it just shifts it into another realm.

Third, although Lewis might criticize the closed system of the - Deists, he ends up with a closed system himself. It is true that his system is bigger than the observable system of natural laws known to man. It is a plurality of systems known to the supernatural power. It is still a system, however, and does not allow for a personal God to supersede his own orderliness with a miracle after the New Testament order.

Conclusion

This author's understanding of miracles can be stated thus:

A miracle is an event which happened when God broke into history and transcended the physical laws which He formulated at creation in order to show Divine sanction to a man or a message.

This understanding allows the following:

First, it shows miracles to be --- not normal or paranormal --- but supernatural.

Second, it affirms the God of the Bible as being the cause.

Third, it shows the purpose as being God's confirmation of the message or messenger.

This definition fits the miracles of the New Testament, but it would not be descriptive of either the supernatural stories of pagans and apostate religions or the counterfeited testimonies of contemporary "miracle workers".

One cannot prove or disprove the miracles of the New Testament. They are too far removed in time and circumstances. One accepts or rejects them because of presuppositions he holds.

The believer accepts them in faith based on the testimony of the Scriptures themselves.[21] This faith is reasonable when one considers the unique nature of the New Testament miracles. They happened for a definite theological purpose --- to confirm men and their messages. They were accepted as genuine by enemies as well as friends. Their nature was such that they could be objectively perceived and tested by those who saw them. There could not have been such a dynamic and enduring faith in the early church if their claim of the miraculous could have been questioned.

The unbeliever rejects the miracles because he has not seen them and cannot prove them. He rejects the testimony of the Scriptures and therefore cannot believe. This unbelief may be rebellious infidelity with its faith in non-faith. It may be sophisticated agnosticism which centers in the limbo of non-affirming doubt. It may even include one with a pious pretense to faith because of sentimental feelings but still has an unwillingness to accept the miracles of the New Testament as being true.

This author begins with faith in the miracles of the Bible and all of the presuppositions which such entails.

ENDNOTES

[1] James R. Ware, *The Sayings of Confusius* (New York: Mentor Books, 1960) p. 82

[2] Acts 2:22

[3] Hebrews 2:4

[4] Matthew 17:6

[5] Luke 4:36; 5:26; 9:43; Acts 3:10; 9:21

[6] Luke 5:26; Acts 3:10

[7] Luke 5:26

[8] John 3:2

[9] Matthew 10:1

[10] Acts 1:8; 2:1ff

[11] Acts 8:19

[12] John 5:20; 9:4; 10:25,32,37,38; 14:10-12; 15:24

[13]John 10:37-38

[14]Colin Brown, *Miracles and the Critical Mind* (Grand Rapids: William B. Eerdmans Publishing Co., 1984) p. 32

[15]William Barclay, *And He Had Compassion on Them* (Edinburgh: Church of Scotland Youth Committee, 1955) p. 5

[16]Brown, *op. cit.*, pp. 47-77

[17]Brown, *op. cit.*, pp. 8-9

[18]C. S. Lewis, *Miracles, a Preliminary Study* (London: Collins Clear Type Press, 1947) p. 9

[19]Lewis, *op. cit.*, p. 6

[20]Lewis, *op. cit.*, p. 13

[21]Romans 10:17; John 20:30-31

CHAPTER 2

THE NEW TESTAMENT MIRACLE NARRATIVES

Classification

There is difficulty in determining the number of miracle narratives in the New Testament. There are three reasons.

First, some events, which the context identifies as being the arbitrary act of God and according to inspired prediction, can be explained as natural happenings.

The coin which Peter found in the fish's mouth is an example of this.[1] Any fisherman knows that all kinds of things can be found in the mouth or stomach of a fish. It is certainly not supernatural every time a coin is found in a fish's mouth. The odds of such a thing happening might be a billion to one. The odds that such would happen at the exact time and place or with the first fish that took Peter's hook would be *ad infinium*. Yet such an event does not suspend the natural laws of the universe. It is a miracle because it was a wondrous event, a *teras*. Its purpose was to show God's sanction of Jesus. It was connected with a prediction which would have been impossible according to natural acquired knowledge.

The great catch of fish on the lake Gennesaret is another example of a miracle not suspending the natural laws of the universe.[2] Any fisherman knows that there are times when it would appear that no fish will be caught. Like Peter who had fished all night, the most diligent effort produced no fish. Then suddenly in the same water many fish

could be caught quickly. The odds of such happening are very great.
The odds of such happening at the same time and place that Jesus said it
would is *ad infinium*. Yet such an event does not suspend the natural
laws of the universe. This event is a miracle because it was a wondrous
act, a *teras* which had as its purpose to show God's sanction of Jesus. It
was also connected with a prediction which would have been impossible
according to naturally acquired knowledge. Experienced fishermen famil-
iar with the erratic patterns of catching fish were seized with amazement
and recognized that the event was from God.[3] The magnitude of the
catch only added to the understanding that the event was a confirming
sign, a *semeion*.

Even though there is nothing in such events which is contrary to
the natural laws of the universe, they are clearly shown to be miracles in
the context. The miraculous element has to do with Divine power
arranging nature to produce wonders as confirming signs to Divinely
sanctioned men and their message. More was involved than guessing -
-- it was foreknowledge. More was involved than chance --- it was God
caused. More was involved than an oddity in nature --- the event had
Divine purpose.

Second, some events are clearly inspired knowledge and foresight
but are not generally included in the miracle lists. To know things
beyond the scope of naturally acquired knowledge and predict happenings before their time clearly involves the miraculous. So much of the
life of Jesus and the activities of the Apostles are entwined with this kind
of thing that it would be difficult to identify each specific event.

Jesus knew the thoughts of Nathanael when he was under the fig
tree.[4] This inspired knowledge was a sufficient sign to Nathanael that he
declared: "Rabbi, You are the Son of God; You are the King of Israel".
This foreknowledge of Jesus was a part of His nature and could not be
separated from any aspect of His life. John commented on this very
thing.

> *But Jesus, on His part, was not entrusting Himself to*
> *them, for He knew all men, and because He did not need any*
> *one to bear witness concerning man for He Himself knew what*
> *was in man.*[5]

Agabus knew that Paul would be imprisoned in Jerusalem.[6] The context shows that this was not just an educated guess but a Divine prediction. Such events as this are not generally listed among the miracle narratives but are clearly wonders wrought by God's power to confirm God's man and message.

Third, some passages tell of miraculous ability given to men but do not relate specific incidents of their use of this ability.

I Corinthians 12 has two lists of spiritual gifts given from God through the Holy Spirit.[7] Fourteen of these gifts are listed. Part of them are clearly of a miraculous nature. The gifts of healing, miracles, distinguishing of spirits, tongues and interpretation of tongues require knowledge or ability that is beyond the natural capacity of man. In these gifts, the normal means by which men do these things were transcended by the direct intervention of God. They could speak and translate languages which they had not studied. They could heal, work miracles and discern spirits with power beyond that acquired by natural ability or acquired knowledge.

Some of the gifts listed in I Corinthians 12 are of a nature that miraculous powers are not always needed. Wisdom, knowledge, faith, prophesy, help, administrations and the role of pastors and teachers do not necessitate miraculous powers. They can exist within the realm of God's natural order of things. By these gifts being listed in this context, it would appear that the apostle wanted to convey that they had some miraculous elements in this case. Wisdom, knowledge and faith are gifts which may be acquired by natural means. They were also given to the Corinthians directly from God in a supernatural way.

These spiritual gifts possessed by the Corinthians would naturally bring about miraculous events. Such are not specifically recorded in the Scriptures. These gifts themselves are miracles but are not generally listed among the New Testament miracles.

The entire scope of New Testament literature flows in and out of the miraculous without attempting to give a formal list of miracles. John records the first formalized miracle of Jesus at the wedding feast in Cana of Galilee.[8] After that some are mentioned, but most are not. At the conclusion of John's Gospel, he summarizes the miracles of Jesus with this statement.

> *Many other signs therefore Jesus also performed in*
> *the presence of the disciples, which are not written in this*

> *book; but these have been written that you may believe
> that Jesus is the Christ, the Son of God; and that believing
> you may have life in His name. . . . .And there are also
> many other things which Jesus did, which if they were
> written in detail, I suppose that even the world itself
> would not contain the books which were written.9*

Jesus' Miracles

A statement made in Halley's Bible Handbook illustrates the difficulty of listing the miracles of Jesus.

> *Aside from supernatural manifestations, such as angelic
> announcements, virgin birth, the star that guided wise men,
> Jesus passing through hostile mobs, cleansing the temple,
> his transfiguration, soldiers falling, darkness at the
> crucifixion, the veil rent, the tombs opened, the earthquake,
> Jesus' resurrection, angel appearances, there are recorded
> 35 miracles which Jesus wrought.10*

Halley's Handbook classifies the miracles under the following headings:

17   Bodily Cures
9   Miracles over Forces of Nature
6   Cures of Demoniacs
3   Raised From the Dead

C. S. Lewis lists thirty-five miracles of Jesus recorded in the four Gospels. Other lists contain more and some lists contain less. The following list will allow the reader to see the number and the recorders of these miraculous events.

Besides these thirty-five specific miracles, there are many general references to Jesus workin miracles.[11]

Miracle:

	Matthew	Mark	Luke	John
Feeding 5,000	14:15-21	6:34-44	9:12-17	6:5-14
Leper Cured	8:1-13	1:40-45	5:12-16	
Peter's mother-in-law cured	8:14-17	1:29-31	4:38-40	
Stilling Storm	8:23-27	4:35-41	8:22-25	
Gadarene Demoniacs	8:28-34	5:1-20	8:26-39	
Paralytic	9:1-8	2:1-12	5:17-26	
Raising of Jairus' Daughter	9:18-26	5:22-43	8:41-56	
Hemorrhaging Woman	9:20-22	5:25-34	8:43-48	
Withered Hand Restored	12:9-13	3:1-5	6:6-11	
Blind Mute	12:22	3:22	11:14	
Epileptic	17:14-21	9:14-29	9:37-42	
Two Blind Men	20:29-34	10:46-52	18:35-43	
Walking on Water	14:22-33	6:45-52		6:15-21
Centurian's Servant	8:5-13		7:1-10	
Syrophoenecian Woman's daughter	15:21-28	7:24-30		
Feeding 4,000	15:23-39	8:1-9		
Fig Tree Cursed	21:18-22	11:12-14		

	Matthew	Mark	Luke	John
Demoniac in Synagogue	1:23-27	4:33-36		
Two Blind men	9:27-31			
Mute Demoniac	9:32-33			
Coin in Fish's mouth	17:24-27			
Deaf Mute		7:31-37		
Blind Man		8:22-26		
Draught of Fish			5:1-11	
Raising of Widow's Son			7:11-16	
Bowed Woman			13:10-17	
Man with Dropsy			14:1-6	
Ten Lepers Cured			17:11-19	
Malchus' Ear Restored		22:49-51		
Water to Wine				2:1-11
Nobleman's Son Cured			4:46-54	
Infirm Man				5:1-16
Man Born Blind				9:1-12
Lazarus Raised				11:10-46
Second Draught of Fish				21:1-23

Literary Aspects of New Testament Miracles

Two things should be observed about the use of the miracle narratives in the New Testament. First, there is a decline of references to miracles from the beginning to the end of the New Testament period. Second, there are different emphases made by the different Gospel writers and different uses made of the miracle narratives.

There is a marked decline of the miraculous events from the time Jesus began his work to the close of the New Testament canon. Both the Synoptics and John are filled with references to the miraculous. From the Divine birth to Jesus' triumphant resurrection, nearly every page of the Gospel affirms the miraculous. Jesus demonstrates His power over nature, over disease, over demons, over sin and over death. A summary of His ministry is given by Matthew.

> *And Jesus was going about in all Galilee, teaching in their synagogues, and proclaiming the gospel of the kingdom, and healing every kind of disease and every kind of sickness among the people. And the news about Him went out into all Syria; and they brought to Him all who were ill, taken with various diseases and pains, demoniacs, epileptics, paralytics; and He healed them.[12]*

At the beginning of the church on the day of Pentecost, the miraculous was prominent. There were people speaking in languages they had never learned, unnatural phenomena like cloven tongues like fire and sound like the rushing of mighty wind. The Apostles spoke inspired words, not from human knowledge, but as the Spirit gave them utterance.[13]

In the first part of Acts, miracles continued to be prominent. There was the healing of the lame man, release from prison and multitudes of signs worked by the Apostles. Then there were miracles in Samaria, Caesarea, Damascus and sprinkled throughout Paul's travels. It should be observed that even in Acts there was a decline in the miracles with the passing of time.

In the epistles there is even a more marked decline in the miraculous. There are references to the abuse of miraculous gifts[14] and the limited purpose and duration of these miraculous gifts[15], but specific references to miracles are rare. There are references to miracles of the past[16]

19

and the inspiration of the writers of the epistles[17], but confirming signs are not evident. There are incidents of uncured illnesses[18] and unrelieved afflictions[19], but no miraculous cures like those Jesus did. There are predictions of the passing of the miraculous gifts[20] and there are warnings of false prophets with false signs[21], but a very conspicuous absence of the kind of mighty works done by Jesus. From the earlier to the later epistles there seems to be a decline in the miraculous.

This phenomenon may be accounted for in three ways:

First, the purposes of the different bodies of literature --- Gospel, Acts and Epistles --- may account for this decline. There would not be so great a need for confirming signs for an Apostolic writing to correct problems in a congregation of believers as there would be to relate the life and teachings of Jesus to an unbelieving world.

Second, the style of epistles and theological tracts is not very conducive to relating miracle stories. The historical narrative of the Gospels and the polemic preaching of Acts would find much greater use for relating miracles.

Third, the decline of the miraculous events in the church is perhaps the best explanation. When the apostles and their immediate circle died and the New Testament documents were completed, it would seem that the miraculous would cease. Their purpose had been fulfilled.

This is perhaps reflected in a passage in Hebrews.

> . . . *How shall we escape if we neglect so great a*
> *salvation? After it was at the first spoken through the Lord,*
> *it was confirmed to us by those who heard, God also bearing*
> *witness with them, both by signs and wonders and by various*
> *miracles and by gifts of the Holy Spirit according to His own*
> *will.[22]*

The passage shows a progression. First, there was that spoken by the Lord. Second, this message was confirmed to the readers by those who heard the Lord. Third, God bore witness to the message of those who heard the Lord with signs, wonders and miracles.

It should be noted that Jesus and the apostles did not work miracles to confirm the Old Testament Scriptures. They had already been confirmed by the miracles worked by Moses and the prophets. Once a thing is confirmed, it does not need to be re-confirmed in every generation.

The message of Moses and the prophets needed no further confirmation by Jesus and the apostles in the New Testament period. In the same way, the message of Jesus and the apostles need no further confirmation in contemporary times.

The decline of miracles from early to the later periods of the New Testament age can best be explained by the fact that the need for miraculous confirmation ceased to exist.

There are different uses of the miracle narratives by the different Gospel writers.

Howard Clark Kee in his book, *Miracles in the Early Christian World*, studies miracles using the sociohistorical method. In his conclusions he writes:

> . . .*The specifics of the event are directly correlated*
> *with the life-world of the writer describing the occurrence,*
> *and that of the reading audience to whom the report is*
> *addressed. The details of the account must be searched to*
> *discover what life-world is presupposed in the narrative*
> *or inscription. . . . .The investigator must at every point raise*
> *contextual and presuppositional questions if the distinctive*
> *function of a miracle --- or any other phenomenon --- is to*
> *be discerned.*[23]

By using this method, Kee suggests that Mark portrays miracles as part of the apocalyptic world view. Matthew and Luke were influenced by literary genres through the historians Suetonius, Tacitus and Josephus. The symbolic nature of miracles is central in the writings of John. He suggests that each of the Gospel writers had a different frame of reference from which he wrote.

Though one might question the theological presuppositions of Kee, his analysis confirms what becomes evident to any careful student of the Gospels. Matthew, Mark, Luke and John wrote from different backgrounds --- life-worlds according to Kee --- and for different purposes and to different audiences. The way miracles are used in their writings reflect this.

Matthew, from a rabbinic Jewish background, uses the miracle narratives to confirm Jesus as the Old Testament Messiah and the fulfillment of Scriptures. Jewish readers would be sensitive to this approach.

Mark, from a more pragmatic, action oriented vantage point, uses the miracle narratives to show the direct power of Jesus' person and His authority. The Roman reader would be more sensitive to this approach.

Luke, from a life-world of Greek literary culture and medical knowledge, uses the miracle narratives to confirm Jesus' work as being the fulfillment of the Old Testament prophecies and a sign of the Kingdom of God. The educated Greek reader would be sensitive to this style and language.

John found symbolic meaning in the miracle narratives. He used them to fulfill his stated purpose in writing . . . "that you may believe". The Jewish reader caught up in the symbols of apocalyptic literature and the readers attracted to the symbols of the Greek Mystery Religions would be sensitive to this approach.

The Acts narrative is to be compared to the Gospel of Luke in its use of the miracles. At the beginning of Acts, Luke uses the miracles on the day of Pentecost to show that the Old Testament Scriptures were being fulfilled[24] and that they were a sign of the Kingdom of God[25].

The use of miracles in the Epistles is rare. This indicates three things.

First, miracles were not needed to show the approval of God for a man or his message. The faith had been established through the New Testament documents and established Apostolic leadership.

Second, the purpose of the Epistles was not to establish new revelation from God, but they were to remind the readers of what they already knew and correct them according to the standards which had already been established.

Third, with the passing of time, many of those individuals who possessed powers to work miracles through the Apostolic office, the baptism of the Holy Spirit and the laying on of apostles' hands had died. Miracles were not so numerous or important.

ENDNOTES

[1]Matthew 17:24-27

[2]Luke 5:1-11, see also John 2:1-11

[3]Luke 5:8-9

[4]John 1:45-50

[5]John 2:24-25

[6]Acts 21:10-1

[7]I Corinthians 12:8-10; 28-30

[8]John 2:1-11

[9]John 20:30-31; 21:25

[10]Henry H. Halley, *Bible Handbook* (Grand Rapids: Zondervan Publishing Co., 1965) p. 469

[11]See Matthew 4:23-24; 9:35; 15:30-31; 19:1-2; Mark 1:32-34; 6:53-56; Luke 4:40; 5:15-16; 6:17-19; 7:21-22; John 2:23; 3:1-2; 4:45; 20:30; 21:25

[12]Matthew 4:23-24

[13]Acts 2:1-4

[14]I Corinthians 12-14

[15]I Corinthians 13:8ff and Ephesians 4:8-13

[16]II Corinthians 12:12

[17]I Corinthians 2:13-16

[18]Philippians 2:25-28

[19]II Corinthians 12:7-10

[20]I Corinthians 13:8 and Ephesians 4:7-13

[21]II Thessalonians 2:8-12; I John 4:1-2

[22]Hebrews 2:3-4

[23]Howard Clark Kee, *Miracles in the Early Christian World* (New Haven: Yale University Press, 1983) p. 293

[24]Acts 2:13

[25]Acts 2:33

Miracles: From God or Man?

CHAPTER 3

MIRACLES IN MATTHEW AND MARK

Each of the Gospel writers uses the miracles of Jesus in a distinct way. The way they use them reflects both their own backgrounds as well as the audience to which they are writing. Matthew and Mark have similarities as well as differences.

Matthew's Use of Miracles

An examination of the miracles recorded in the Gospel of Matthew shows that there are nine general references to miracles, ten times in which references are made to inspiration or direct acts from God and twenty times in which a specific miracle of Jesus is recorded. The following chart shows these references.

Matthew's Miracles:

I. General References (10)

4:23-24	14:14
8:16	14:35-36
9:35	15:30-31
11:4-5	19:1-2
12:15	21:14

II. Inspiration and Direct Acts from God (10)

1:20-21	An Angel visits Joseph
2:2	Appearance of the Star
2:12	Dream of the Wise Men
2:13-14	Dream of Joseph to Flee to Egypt
2:19-21	Dream of Joseph to Return to Nazareth
3:16-17	Spirit as Dove and Voice at Jesus' Baptism
4:1-11	Temptation of Devil and Ministry of Angels
17:1-8	Transfiguration
27:51-54	Earthquake, Resurrection of Saints and Veil Rent
28:1-2	Earthquake and Angels at Resurrection

III. Miracles of Jesus (20)

8:2-4	Healed a Leper
8:5-13	Healed a Centurian's Servant
8:14-15	Healed Peter's Mother-in-law
8:23-27	Stilled the Storm
8:28-34	Cast Demons into Swine on Coast of Gadarenes
9:2-5	Healed a Paralytic
9:18-25	Raised the Daughter of a Synagogue Official
9:20-22	Healed Woman with Hemorrhage
9:27-30	Healed Two Blind Men
9:32-33	Healed Dumb Demoniac
12:10-13	Healed Man with a Withered Hand
12:22	Healed the Blind and Dumb Demoniac
14:15-21	Fed the 5,000
14:23-32	Walked on Water
15:21-28	Cast Demon from the Daughter of Canaanite Woman
15:32-38	Fed the 4,000
17:14-18	Healed Epileptic Demoniac Boy
17:27	Peter Caught Fish with Coin in Its Mouth
20:29-34	Healed Two Blind Men near Jericho
21:18-20	Cursed the Barren Fig Tree

Matthew's Gospel is arranged in a more topical way than the other three. There are sections on the sayings of Jesus, the parables, judgment and miracles. Chapters eight and nine contain one half of the miracles recorded in the book --- ten out of twenty. In these chapters are hints of the purposes that Matthew has in using the miracle narratives. There are three.

First, Matthew sees Jesus' miracles as a fulfillment of the Messianic predictions made in the Old Testament Scriptures. Jesus is the fulfillment of the Suffering Servant of Isaiah 53.

> *And when evening had come, they brought to Him many*
> *who were demon-possessed; and He cast out the spirits with*
> *a word, and healed all who were ill; in order that what was*
> *spoken through Isaiah the prophet might be fulfilled, saying,*
> *He Himself took our infirmities, and carried away our*
> *diseases[1].*

Jesus' desire to avoid publicity is a fulfillment of Isaiah 42:1-4. Matthew used this as the reason that Jesus asked those He healed not to make it known.

> *But Jesus, aware of this, withdrew from there. And many*
> *followed Him, and He healed them all, and warned them*
> *not to make Him known; in order that what was spoken*
> *through Isaiah the prophet, might be fulfilled, saying,*
> *Behold, my servant whom I have chosen; my*
> *beloved in whom my soul is well pleased; I will put*
> *my spirit upon him, and he shall proclaim justice to*
> *the Gentiles. He will not quarrel, nor cry out; nor*
> *will any one hear his voice in th estreets. A battered*
> *reed he will not break off, and a smoldering wick he*
> *will not put out, until he leads justice to victory[2].*

When John sent his disciples to Jesus to inquire if He were the coming one, Jesus responded by quoting a medley of Scriptures from Isaiah.

> *And Jesus answered and said to them, Go and report to John*
> *the things which you hear and see: the **blind receive sight***
> *and the lame walk, the lepers are cleansed and the deaf hear,*
> *and the dead are raised up, and the **poor have the gospel***
> *preached to them[3].*

27

Second, Matthew sees Jesus' power for physically healing the sick as a confirmation of His spiritual power to forgive sins and defeat Satan. He told the paralytic which was lowered through the roof in order to get near him, "My son, your sins are forgiven". The scribes who heard Him criticized Him and accused Him of blasphemy. Jesus' response was:

> *For which is easier, to say, 'Your sins are forgiven,' or to say, 'Rise, and walk'? But in order that you may know that the Son of Man has authority on earth to forgive sins --- then He said to the paralytic, 'Rise, take up your bed, and go home'[4].*

After healing the blind and dumb demoniac, the Pharisees accused Jesus of casting out demons by Beelzebul. His response to them was that such was impossible since, "a kingdom divided against itself is laid waste". Satan would not fight against himself would he? Yet that would be the case if Jesus cast out demons by the prince of demons. On the other hand, Jesus argues:

> *But if I cast out demons by the Spirit of God, then the kingdom of God has come upon you. Or how can anyone enter the strong man's house and carry off his property, unless he first binds the strong man? And then he will plunder his house[5].*

Jesus' spiritual power over the devil is confirmed by His physical power to cast out demons.

Third, Matthew sees Jesus' miracles as demonstrations of His compassion. He healed the undesirables of His day --- the lepers[6], a centurian's slave[7], two demon-possessed men[8], a paralytic[9], and the blind and dumb man[10]. One of the summary statements Matthew makes of Jesus' ministry emphasizes compassion.

> *And Jesus was going about all the cities and villages, teaching in their synagogues, and proclaiming the gospel of the kingdom, and healing every kind of disease and every kind of sickness. And seeing the multitudes, He felt compassion for them, because they were distressed and downcast like sheep without a shepherd.[11]*

It is Matthew that records the two times Jesus quotes from Hosea 6:6, "I desire compassion and not sacrifice"[12]. In both passages, Jesus is shown to have compassion for those who were scorned by the Pharisees.

Four times in the context of working a miracle, Matthew says that Jesus felt compassion.[13] Mark and Luke record only one time each that Jesus felt compassion.[14]

Matthew wanted his readers not only to see the miracles of Jesus as being Divine confirmation of His spiritual power and the fulfillment of the Messianic predictions of the Old Testament Scriptures, but he also wanted them to know the feelings of compassion which Jesus had for the afflicted.

Matthew records the sayings of Jesus which expose the wrong motives for seeking signs from heaven.

The Pharisees refused to accept Jesus or His miracles as being from God. They accused Him of casting out demons by Beelzebul.[15] In Jesus' response to their accusations, He exposed their evil hearts.

> *You brood of vipers, how can you, being evil, speak what is good? For the mouth speaks out of that which fills the heart.[16]*

The Pharisees along with the scribes, in spite of the fact that they had just seen Jesus cast a demon out of a blind and dumb man, said, "Teacher, we want to see a sign from you". Jesus' answer was sharp and clear.

> *But He answered and said to them, 'An evil and adulterous generation craves for a sign; and yet no sign shall be given to it but the sign of Jonah the prophet'.[17]*

Signs do not do any good for those who do not want to believe. Jesus refused to satisfy the curiosity of those who had bad hearts.

After the feeding of the 4,000 the Pharisees and Sadducees came to Jesus and asked Him to show them a sign from heaven.[18] They were testing Jesus to see if He, like Moses, would give bread from heaven. Their test was: "If you are a new Moses, then give us manna as he did". He had just fed the 4,000, but to one who chooses not to believe, no proof is enough. Jesus refused to be manipulated by their insincere requests and replied:

> *An evil and adulterous generation seeks after a sign; and*
> *a sign will not be given it, except the sign of Jonah. And He*
> *left them, and went away.[19]*

Matthew warns against false miracle workers. In the closing part of the
sermon on the mount, Matthew alone records the words of Jesus:

> *Not every one who says to Me, Lord, Lord, will enter the*
> *kingdom of heaven; but he who does the will of My Father,*
> *who is in heaven. Many will say to Me on that day, Lord,*
> *Lord, did we not prophesy in Your name, and in Your name cast*
> *out demons, and in Your name perform many miracles? And*
> *then I will declare to them, I never knew you; Depart from me,*
> *you who practice lawlessness.[20]*

Jesus clearly says there will be men who will claim to know Him and
work miracles in His name but are rejected by him. Confessing Jesus'
Lordship and claiming miracles in Jesus' name are empty and void without faithful obedience.

Matthew, along with Mark, records the words of Jesus in the
Apocalyptic section on the destruction of the temple and the sign of
Jesus' coming. In times of peril, there will always be false prophets.
Jesus warns of such.

> *For false Christs and false prophets will arise and will*
> *show great signs and wonders, so as to mislead, if possible,*
> *even the elect.[21]*

This prophecy of Jesus has been fulfilled in every generation since that
time. False Christs and false prophets still make claims of miracles.

Mark's Use of Miracles

An examination of the miracles recorded in the Gospel of Mark shows
that there are five general references to miracles, five times when inspiration or a direct act of God is recorded and eighteen specific miracles.
The following chart lists these categories.

Mark's Miracles

I. General References (6)

1:32-34	6:5
1:39	6:55-56
3:10-11	16:17-20

II. Inspiration and Direct Acts from God (5)

1:9-11	Dove and Voice from Heaven at Baptism
1:12-13	Temptation of Devil and Ministry of Angels
9:2-8	Transfiguration
9:38	Renting of Veil of Temple
16:12	Jesus' appearance to two disciples

III. Miracles of Jesus (18)

1:23-27	Cast out Demon at Synagogue in Capernaum
1:30-31	Healed Peter's Mother-in-law
1:40-42	Healed a Leper
2:3-12	Healed a Paralytic
3:1-5	Healed a Man with a Withered Hand
4:35-39	Stilled the Storm
5:1-13	Cast Demons into Swine
5:22-42	Raised Jairus' Daughter
5:25-34	Healed Woman with Hemorrhage
6:34-44	Fed 5,000
6:47-51	Walked on Water
7:24-30	Cast Demon from the Daughter of Syrophoenican Woman
7:32-37	Healed Deaf and Dumb Man
8:1-9	Fed 4,000
8:22-25	Healed Blind Man at Bethsaida
9:17-29	Cast Demons from Demoniac Boy
10:46-52	Healed Blind Bartimaeus at Jericho
11:12-14	Cursed Barren Fig Tree

Mark's account of the miracles of Jesus are similar to Matthew's. He recorded nineteen miracles with all but three being the same as Matthew.[22]

With Mark, there is an emphasis on Jesus, the one with personal power and authority to work wonders. A summary statement that he gives of Jesus' ministry suggests this.

> *And wherever He entered villages, or cities, or countryside,*
> *they were laying the sick in the marketplaces, and entreating*
> *Him that they might just touch the fringe of His cloak; and*
> *as many as touched it were cured.[23]*

Jesus' power was so great that merely touching the fringe of His garment would heal.

Mark emphasizes the public nature of Jesus' healing ministry: the whole city had gathered together;[24] they were coming to him from everywhere;[25] many were gathered together;[26] all the multitude were coming to Him;[27] a great multitude heard of all that He was doing and came to Him.[28] All of these expressions used by Mark emphasizes the popularity of Jesus' mighty works.

There seems to be an emphasis in Mark on Jesus' personal touch. To touch or be touched by Jesus was an important part of the miracle.

> *For He had healed many, with the result that all those*
> *who had afflictions pressed about Him in order to touch*
> *Him.[29]*

The woman with a hemorrhage "touched Him".[30] The people sought to "touch" His cloak and those who did were healed.[31] He laid His hands upon a few sick people and healed them.[32] The blind man from Bethsaida asked to be "touched" by Jesus.[33]

The two healings which are unique to Mark focus on Jesus putting His fingers into the ears, touching the tongue and laying hands on the eyes of the afflicted.[34]

Even in the mission He gave to the twelve, there is "anointing with oil" connected with healing. In the great commission according to Mark, the Gospel was to be confirmed with the sign of healing which was accompanied by "laying hands on the sick".

Like Matthew, Mark shows that one of the purposes of miracles was to confirm Jesus' spiritual power to forgive sins.[35]

Like Matthew, Mark sees the miracles of Jesus as an expression of His compassion.[36]

Unlike Matthew, Mark does not show the miracles as a fulfillment of the Old Testament Messianic prophecies.

This should be compared to the fact that the Old Testament is hardly referred to in Mark while it is directly quoted thirty-eight times in Matthew. Matthew has a Jewish genealogy, but Mark has none.

Mark shows the miracles as being a demonstration of Jesus' power and authority. This distinctive feature in Mark may reflect a primary destination of the Gospel as being the Roman culture which focused on power and authority.

Mark is very clear in showing the purpose of miracles as being for the confirmation of the Gospel.[37]

> *And these signs will accompany those who have believed:*
> *in My name they will cast out demons, they will speak with new*
> *tongues; they will pick up serpents, and if they drink any*
> *deadly poison, it shall not hurt them; they will lay hands*
> *on the sick, and they will recover . . . . .And they went out and*
> *preached everywhere, while the Lord worked with them, and*
> *confirmed the word by the signs that followed.[38]*

This confirmation of the word by miracles was to be wherever the Gospel was preached and for all time. It was not limited to Palestine in the apostolic age. This is made clear by the language of the text.

Signs would accompany "those who have believed", but who are these believers?

Are they the apostles who were reproached for their unbelief? Verse 14 says, "He reproached them for their unbelief and hardness of heart, because they had not believed those who had seen Him after He had risen". Because of this some would suggest that miracles were only to follow the apostles in their preaching.

Are "those who have believed" to be understood as all believers for all time? Verse 16 says, "He who has believed and has been baptized shall be saved; but he who has disbelieved shall be condemned".

Because this passage comes immediately before the promise that "these signs will accompany those who have believed", some would suggest that the miracles would accompany all baptized believers for all time.

The latter is true. Signs will accompany all believers for all time. One can know that this is the meaning because of the grammar. In the text, when Jesus refers to Himself, it was in the first person. When He refers to the apostles, He used the second person. When He used the third person, it referred to those believers who had been baptized. The third person was used when Jesus says that "signs would follow those who believed".

It should be noted that the text does not say that signs would be "worked" by those who believed.[39] It says that signs would "accompany" those who believed. They do because wherever and whenever the Gospel is preached, the signs that Jesus did are also told. John said that the purpose of writing about the signs was to make men believe.[40] The multitude of signs and miracles recorded in the New Testament are still accompanying the preaching of the Gospel.

Mark comments on this promise of Jesus in the last verse of the Gospel.

> . . . *the Lord worked with them, and confirmed the word*
> *by the signs that followed.[41]*

He plainly states that the signs were for confirmation of the word preached. He then adds that such was experienced in the preaching of the Gospel in his time. Those same signs that were experienced and witnessed by apostolic writers are still confirming the word. There is no new Gospel and there are no new signs.

ENDNOTES

[1]Matthew 8:16-17

[2]Matthew 12:15-20

[3]Matthew 11:4-5

[4]Matthew 9:4-5

[5]Matthew 12:28-29

[6]Matthew 8:2-4

[7]Matthew 8:5-13

[8]Matthew 8:25

[9]Matthew 9:2-5

[10]Matthew 12:12

[11]Matthew 9:35-36

[12]Matthew 9:13; 12:7

[13]Matthew 9:36; 14:14; 15:32; 20:34

[14]Mark 1:11 and Luke 7:13

[15]Matthew 12:22-24

[16]Matthew 12:34

[17]Matthew 12:39

[18]Matthew 16:1

[19]Matthew 16:4

[20]Matthew 7:21-23

[21]Matthew 24:24

[22]Mark 1:23; 7:31-37; 8:22-26

[23]Mark 6:56

[24]Mark 1:33

[25]Mark 1:45

[26]Mark 2:2

[27]Mark 2:13

[28]Mark 3:8

[29]Mark 3:10

[30]Mark 5:25

[31]Mark 6:56

[32]Mark 6:5

[33]Mark 8:22

[34]Mark 7:31-37; 8:22-26

[35]Mark 2:10-11

[36]Mark 1:41; 6:34; 8:2

[37]For a discussion of the testual problems involved in the ending of Mark see Jimmy Jividen, *Glossolalia* (Fort Worth: Star Bible Publications, 1971) pp. 89-98

[38]Mark 16:17-18

[39]*parakolouthesei* is used in verse 17 concerning the signs which were to follow. *Epakolouthounton* is used in verse 20 to speak of the signs which did follow the apostles in their preaching

[40]John 20:31

[41]Mark 16:20

CHAPTER 4

MIRACLES IN LUKE AND JOHN

It is artificial to bring Luke and John together in one chapter since they make such diverse use of the miracle narratives. Luke could be easily connected to Acts. John could well form a chapter of its own because it is so distinctive.

They are considered together in this study to balance out the quanity of the miracle material with Matthew and Mark in this presentation. The material of this chapter is divided into two separate sections.

Luke's Use of Miracles

An examination of the miracles recorded in the Gospel of Luke shows that there are six general references to miracles, eighteen times in which references are made to inspiration or direct acts from God and twenty-one times in which specific miracles of Jesus are recorded. The following chart shows these references.

Luke's Miracles:

I. General References (6)

4:5	6:17-19
4:40-41	7:21
5:15	9:11

II. Inspiration and Direct Acts from God (18)

1:11-22	Angel to Zacharias
1:20-22	Zacharias Struck Dumb
1:26-38	Angel to Mary
1:41-45	Inspired Praise of Elizabeth
1:46-55	Inspired Praise of Mary
1:64	Zacharias Healed from Dumbness
1:67-79	Inspired Prophecy of Zacharias
2:9-15	Angels to Shepherds
2:25-32	Inspired Prophecy of Simeon
2:36-38	Inspired Prophecy of Anna
3:21-22	Spirit as Dove and Voice at Jesus' Baptism
4:1-12	Temptation of Devil
9:28-36	Transfiguration
23:44-45	Sun Darkened and Veil Rent
24:1-7,23	Angel to Women at Tomb
24:13-31	Jesus' Appearance before Two Men on Way to Emmaus
24:36	Jesus Appeared to Apostles
24:50-51	Ascension of Jesus

III. Miracles of Jesus (21)

4:28-30	Escape from Mob at Nazareth
4:31-36	Casts out Demon at Capernaum
4:38-39	Healed Peter's Mother-in-law
5:4-9	Draught of Fish
5:12-14	Healed a Leper
5:17-26	Healed a Paralytic
6:6-11	Healed Man with Withered Hand
7:1-10	Healed Centurian's Slave at Capernaum
7:11-17	Raised the Son of the Widow of Nain
8:22-25	Stills the Storm
8:26-39	Casts Demons into Swine
8:41-56	Raised Jairus' Daughter
8:43-48	Healed Woman with Hemorrhage

9:12-17	Fed 5,000
9:38-43	Casts Demon from Demoniac Boy
11:14-15	Heals Dumb Demoniac
13:11-12	Heals Woman Bent Double by Spirit
14:2-4	Heals Man with Dropsy
17:12-16	Heals Ten Lepers
18:35-43	Heals Blind Man near Jericho
22:50-51	Heals Malchus' Ear

Luke's account of Jesus' life contains the greatest number of miracles. The use of these miracles in his writings reflects both his purpose and the nature of the audience to whom it was directed.

Luke has a particular interest in the miracles of healing. Of the twenty-two miracles he records, sixteen deal with physical healing. Since Luke is described as a physician by Paul, one would expect this emphasis. William Hobart in his book, *Medical Language of Luke*, shows that the Gospel of Luke contains technical medical language, particularly in the healing miracles of Jesus.[1]

The literary style of Luke is distinctive from other New Testament writings. Howard Clark Kee observes that this distinction is due to his knowledge of Graeco-Roman culture and his familiarity with the methods of the Hellenistic historian.

> *Fundamental to all that Luke writes is his knowledge of Graeco-Roman culture and his ability to exploit that familiarity to enhance the effectiveness of his propagandistic undertaking. Henry J. Cadbury's classic studies of the style and literary methods of Luke showed . . . that Luke was familiar with the methods of Hellenistic historians and adapted them to serve his own ends.[2]*

The prologue of Luke contains the most classical Greek style of all of the New Testament.[3] Luke's second volume, Acts, is structured and composed according to the style of a Greek historian. Luke emphasizes the universality of Jesus' message. These factors and others would cause one to expect a distinct use of the miracle narratives in the Gospel.

The first purpose of miracles in Luke appears to be that they are signs of fulfilled Messianic prophecy from the Old Testament. Two passages reflect this.

On the occasion of Jesus' reading the scroll in the synagogue of Nazareth, He chooses a passage from Isaiah 61:1-2. Luke records His reading.

> *The Spirit of the Lord is upon me, because he*
> *anointed me to preach the gospel to the poor. He has*
> *sent me to proclaim release to the captives, and to set*
> *free those who are downtrodden, to proclaim the*
> *favorable year of the Lord.[4]*

When Jesus finished reading He sat down and said: "Today this Scripture has been fulfilled in your hearing". The miracles predicted in Isaiah 61 were fulfilled in the work of Jesus. Luke sees this as one of the purposes of miracles.

On the occasion of the messengers of John inquiring if He were the coming Messiah, Jesus responds with a medley of Scriptures taken from Isaiah.[5] His answer was as follows:

> . . .*Go and report to John what you have seen and heard:*
> *the blind receive sight, the lame walk, the lepers are*
> *cleansed, the deaf hear, the dead are raised up, the poor*
> *have the gospel preached to them.[6]*

Jesus showed that He indeed was the fulfillment of the Messianic prophecies because of His healing ministry.

A second purpose in Luke's use of the miracle narratives has already been identified in Matthew and Mark. They confirm Jesus' spiritual power to forgive sins by demonstrating His power to heal the physically sick.[7]

A third purpose in Luke's use of the miracle narratives is that they are a sign of the kingdom. Jesus, in denying that He casts out demons by the power of Beelzebul, affirmed that He did so by the "finger of God". This is identified as being a sign of the Kingdom of God.

> *But if I cast out demons by the finger of God, then the*
> *kingdom of God has come upon you.[8]*

It should be observed that Luke emphasized the response that people made to the miracles of Jesus. People responded with amazement, awe,

marvel and fear.9 An example of this emphasis is shown in Luke's
account of the healing of the paralytic.

> *And they were all seized with astonishment and began*
> *glorifying God; and they were filled with fear, saying,*
> *'We have seen remarkable things today'.10*

The people who observed the miracles knew that something supernatural
was taking place. They were astonished because it was a wonder. They
were filled with fear and awe because they did not understand it. They
knew a remarkable thing had happened, and they glorified God who was
the source of it.

In spite of the emphasis Luke gives to miracles, he records the
teachings of Jesus about things which are greater than miracles.

When the seventy returned from their healing and preaching ministry, they rejoiced that even the demons were subject to the power they
received from Jesus. Jesus told them that there were things which were
greater than this miraculous power.

> *And the seventy returned with joy, saying, 'Lord, even the*
> *demons are subject to us in Your name'. And He said to them,*
> *'I was watching Satan fall from heaven like lightning. Behold,*
> *I have given you authority to tread upon serpents and*
> *scorpions, and over all the power of the enemy, and nothing*
> *shall injure you. Nevertheless do not rejoice in this, that*
> *the spirits are subject to you, but rejoice that your names*
> *are recorded in heaven . . . . for I say to you, that many*
> *prophets and kings wished to see the things which you see,*
> *and did not see them, and to hear the things which you hear,*
> *and did not hear them'.11*

The text shows that there are at least two things which are greater than the
miracles which the seventy had received.

First, they should rejoice more because their names were recorded
in heaven than they did over the power to cast out demons. This was
greater than miracles.

Second, they should rejoice because they had heard and seen
things which kings and prophets had not known. This was greater than
miracles.

John's Use of Miracles

An examination of the miracles recorded in the Gospel of John shows that there are seven general references to miracles, ten times there are references to inspiration or direct acts from God and eight times specific miracles of Jesus are recorded.

John's Miracles:

I. General References (7)

2:23	7:31
3:2	20:30-31
4:45	21:25
6:2	

II. Inspiration and Direct Acts from God (10)

1:32-33	Spirit as Dove at Baptism
1:45-48	Jesus Saw Nathanael under Fig Tree
4:17,19,39	Jesus Knew the Past of the Samaritan Woman
11:50-51	Caiaphas Prophesied of Jesus
12:29	Voice from Heaven
14:29	Jesus Predicted his Death
20:12	Two Angels at the Tomb
20:19	Jesus Appeared in Midst of Disciples
20:26	Jesus Appeared in Midst of Disciples with Door Closed
21:1	Jesus Manifested Himself at Sea of Tiberias

III. Miracles of Jesus (8)

2:1-11	Changes Water into Wine
4:46:54	Healed Nobleman's Son
5:1-9	Healed Lame Man at Bethesda Pool
6:5-14	Fed 5,000

6:15-21	Walks on Water
9:1-12	Heals Man born Blind
11:11-46	Raised Lazarus
21:4-8	Draught of Fish

The Gospel of John is unique in its use of miracles in several ways.

First, it contains the fewest number of miracles. There are only eight. Only two of these eight --- the feeding of the 5,000 and walking on water --- are recorded in the Synoptics. The other six are unique to John.

Second, two words are used by John for the miracles of Jesus -- signs and works. John's favorite word was "sign". It means, "to point to something beyond itself". In the case of John's Gospel, the signs pointed to Jesus and were for the purpose of producing faith in those who saw them. This is so stated by John, "these have been written that you may believe".[12] John selected a few of the many miraculous signs Jesus worked to be included in the Gospel.

And there are also many other things which Jesus did, which
if they were written in detail, I suppose that even the world
itself would not contain the books which were written.[13]

The signs done by Jesus were done in the presence of His disciples.

They were eye witnesses. John gives His personal witness that these signs are true and authentic.

This is the disciple who bears witness of these things, and
wrote these things; and we know that his witness is true.[14]

The purpose of the signs was to produce faith. The primary purpose was not benevolent acts of kindness or compassion for the suffering. The purpose was to cause men to believe.

The purpose was not a public relations tool to gain acclaim and get a popular following. Jesus' brothers appear to desire this purpose, but Jesus rejected their counsel.

His brothers therefore said to Him, 'Depart from here,
go into Judea, that Your disciples also may behold Your works
which You are doing. For no one does anything in secret,

when he himself seeks to be known publicly. If You do
these things, Show Yourself to the world'.15

Jesus' response to them was, "My time is not yet at hand".
     The purpose was not for physical comfort or ease. This view
seemed to be held by some who had witnessed the feeding of the 5,000.

They said therefore to Him, 'What then do You do for a sign,
that we may see, and believe You? What works do You perform?
Our fathers ate manna in the wilderness: as it is written,
He gave them bread out of heaven to eat.16

They liked the idea of having bread for which they did not labor. If Jesus
would provide this, they were all for Him. Jesus knew their motive for
desiring signs and would not do what they wanted. He said,

Truly, truly, I say to you, you seek Me, not because you saw
signs, but because you ate of the loaves, and were filled.17

Most of Jesus' contemporaries failed to see the signs for what they were -
-- a confirmation of His person and His message. Who Jesus claimed to
be could not be separated from the works which He did. Jesus said, "the
works that I do in My Father's name, these bear witness to Me".18 Those
who witnessed the miracles could not deny that they were genuine. If
they were genuine, then Jesus must be who He claimed to be.
     The blind man that Jesus healed, asked the Pharisees, "How can a
man who is a sinner perform such signs?"19 Others were saying, "a
demon can not open the eyes of the blind, can he?".20
     Even Jesus' enemies could not deny His miracles. They lived
with a contradiction. They knew His miracles were genuine, but they
refused to believe He was who He said He was. This dilemma is
reflected in a statement in the Gospel.

Therefore the chief priests and the Pharisees convened a
council, and were saying, 'What are we doing? For this man
is performing many signs. If we let Him go on like this, all
men will believe in Him'.21

They could not discredit His work, they sought to destroy Him. The counsel of Caiaphas was, "It is expedient for you that one man should die for the people".[22]

Nicodemus recognized that the signs were real and served to confirm that God was with Jesus. He said, "Rabbi, we know that you have come from God, as a teacher; for no one can do these signs that You do unless God is with him".[23]

Even the rejection of Jesus' signs was a confirmation of His Messiahship. Isaiah prophesied that He would be rejected, so His very rejection confirmed that He was the One Who was to come. John makes this point in commenting on the unbelief of the Jews.

> *But though He had performed so many signs before them,*
> *yet they were not believing in Him, that the word of Isaiah*
> *the prophet might be fulfilled, which he spoke, 'Lord who*
> *has believed our report?" And to whom has the*
> *arm of the Lord been revealed?" For this cause they could*
> *not believe, for Isaiah said again, He has blinded their eyes,*
> *and hardended their heart . . .* [24]

The purpose of miracles in the Gospel of John is clear. The unbelief of the Jews is just as clear. Throughout the Gospel there is tension. On the one hand there were the witness of John the Baptist, the signs that Jesus worked, and the testimony of the Scriptures themselves.[25] On the other hand there was the rejection of the Jews in unbelief. They could not deny His works, so they sought to destroy His person.

The summary statement of John's Gospel affirms the confirming purpose of miracles.

> *Many other signs therefore Jesus also performed in the*
> *presence of the disciples, which are not written in this*
> *book; but these have been written that you may believe that*
> *Jesus is the Christ, the Son of God.*[26]

Also unique with the miracles in John is their symbolic nature.. John uses the physical signs to illustrate spiritual lessons.

In the feeding of the 5,000, Jesus used physical bread as a symbol to talk about the bread of life.[27]

In healing the man born blind, He taught a lesson on spiritual blindness.[28] When He raised Lazarus from the dead, He taught that "I am the resurrection and the life".[29]   *45*

The parables of Jesus were about common physical things. He used them to teach spiritual truth.

The fact that John used miracles as symbols to teach does not diminish from their historical reality. Jesus used the factual realities of nature to illustrate spiritual truths in the parables. It did not diminish from the reality of nature because He used them to teach a spiritual lesson. In the same way, He used the factual realities of His miracles to illustrate spiritual truths. It did not diminish from their factual reality because He used them to teach a spiritual truth.

ENDNOTES

[1] William Kirk Hobart, *The Medical Language of St. Luke* (Grand Rapids: Baker Book House, 1954) p. xxix

[2] Howard Clark Kee, *Miracles in the Early Christian World* (New Haven: Yale University Press, 1983) p. 190

[3] Luke 1:1-4

[4] Luke 4:18-19

[5] Isaiah 29:18-19; 35:5-6; 61:1

[6] Luke 7:22

[7] Luke 5:24

[8] Luke 11:22

[9] Luke 4:36; 5:8-9, 26; 7:16-17; 8:25, 56; 9:43; 11:14

[10] Luke 5:26

[11] Luke 10:17-20, 24

[12] John 20:31

[13] John 21:25

[14] John 21:24

[15] John 7:3-4

[16] John 6:30-31

[17]John 6:26

[18]John 10:25

[19]John 9:16

[20]John 10:21

[21]John 11:47

[22]John 11:50

[23]John 3:2

[24]John 12:37-40

[25]John 5:33-39

[26]John 20:30-31a

[27]John 6:48

[28]John 9:39-40

[29]John 11:25

Miracles: From God or Man?

CHAPTER 5

MIRACLES IN ACTS

Acts is the second volume of Luke's writings. The similarities that it has with his Gospel are not only in style and language but also in its use of the miracles.

It has already been stated that there is a decline in the miraculous from the Gospels to Acts. There is even a greater decline in the miraculous from Acts to the Epistles. There is also a noticeable decline from the beginning chapters of Acts to the close of the book.

A careful reading of Acts reveals that there are ten general references to miracles, twenty references to inspiration or a direct act of God and eleven miracles worked by the apostles. The following chart identifies them.

Miracles in Acts:

I. General References (10)

2:43	8:6-8,13
4:30	14:3
5:12	15:12
5:15-16	19:11-12
6:8	28:9

II. Inspiration and Direct Acts from God (20)

     1:3   Appearance to Disciples after Resurrection

1:9	Ascension
2:1-6	Four Miracles on the Day of Pentecost
4:31	Place Shaken after Prayer
5:19	Peter Released from Prison
8:26	Angel Spoke to Philip
9:1-9	Light and Voice on Saul's Journey to Damascus
9:12	Ananias' Vision
10:3	Cornelius' Vision
10:10-23	Peter's Trance Concerning Gentiles
10:19	Spirit Directs Peter to Go to Cornelius
10:46	Cornelius and His Household Speak in Tongues
11:28	Agabus' Prophecy Concerning Famine
12:5	Peter Delivered from Prison
12:23	Herod's Death
14:19-20	Paul Restored to Life after Being Stoned
16:6	Paul Forbidden to Preach in Asia
16:9	Vision to Go to Macedonia
21:10-12	Agabus' Prophecy Concerning Paul's Imprisonment
27:23-26	Angel's Message to Paul Concerning Shipwreck

III. Miracles of the Apostles (12)

3:1-10	Lame Man Healed
5:1-11	Ananias and Sapphira Struck Dead
9:12-17	Saul Healed from Blindness
9:32-35	Healing of Aeneas
9:40-42	Dorcas Raised from Dead
13:6-12	Elymas Struck Blind
14:8-10	Lame Man Healed
16:16-17	Demon Cast Out of Damsel
19:6	Twelve Men Spoke in Tongues and Prophesied
20:9-12	Eutychus Restored to Life
28:3-5	Healing of Viper Bite on Paul
28:8-9	Publius' Father Healed

Means of the Miraculous

The Acts narrative shows that miracles were performed in different ways. Some were direct from God, like the four which were witnessed on the day of Pentecost.[1] Some were worked through the hands of the apostles.[2] Some were performed through only a shadow of Peter or a handkerchief or apron from Paul.[3] Some were worked by those who had received the laying on of apostles' hands.[4]

It should be observed that all of the miracles in Acts which were done by men were done by either the apostles or those who had received, or could have received, the laying on of the apostles' hands. Luke clearly identifies the apostles as having power to work miracles.

> *And at the hands of the apostles many signs and wonders were taking place among the people.*[5]

This statement comes immediately after Ananias and Sapphira had tried to deceive the apostles and were struck dead by God.[6] God confirmed the apostles as His messengers with a miracle. This caused the people to hold them in high esteem.[7]

The apostles were connected with most of the miracles in Acts which were worked by men. The exceptions were those worked by Stephen and Philip and the restoring of Saul's sight by Ananias.[8] Even Stephen and Philip had received the laying on of the apostles' hands when they were chosen as servants in the church at Jerusalem.[9]

The apostolic office carried with it power and authority. The apostles had been promised and had received the baptism of the Holy Spirit.[10] Paul asserted his authority in his epistles by affirming his apostleship. There must have been some kind of demonstrable power in this office since Paul speaks of apostolic signs.

> *The signs of a true apostle were performed among you with all perseverance, by signs and wonders and miracles.*[11]

The power of the apostolic office did not come through the baptism of the Holy Spirit. It was inherent in the office itself. The apostles had been called and trained by Jesus. They had participated in His work of healing and preaching. They had received a commission to preach the Gospel. They had been given the Holy Spirit even before the baptism of the Holy

Spirit on the day of Pentecost.[12] The apostolic office was a distinctive gift to certain men.[13]

The New Testament also uses the term "apostle" in a generic sense. The term literally means "one sent". It sometimes refers to others besides those chosen by Jesus for a special office. The twelve and Paul were special "apostles of Jesus Christ". They were "sent" on a special mission by Jesus Christ Himself. The term refers to others who were also sent.

Jesus is called an "apostle". He was "one sent from God".[14] Moses was an "apostle". He was "one sent" from God on a special mission.[15] It seems that Barnabas was referred to as an apostle.[16] He was "sent out" by the church.

One must not confuse the generic use of the term "apostle" with its special use in referring to the apostolic office in the New Testament.

Cornelius and his household received the baptism of the Holy Spirit, but not the apostolic office.[17] There is no evidence that they had any power to give the Holy Spirit through the laying on of hands.

The apostles could work miracles because of their apostolic office. God confirmed these men and their message through signs, wonders and miracles.

Luke also identifies the special power which came through the the apostles' hands.

> *Now when the apostles in Jerusalem heard that Samaria had received the word of God, they sent them Peter and John, who came down and prayed for them, that they might receive the Holy Spirit. For He had not yet fallen upon any of them; they had simply been baptized in the name of the Lord Jesus. Then they began laying their hands on them, and they were receiving the Holy Spirit. Now when Simon saw that the Spirit was bestowed through the laying on of the apostles' hands . . .[18]*

Miracles were sometimes connected with those who did not receive the laying on of the apostles' hands in Acts. In these cases, the individuals were connected to the miracle in a passive way.

These individuals received the visitation of angels.[19] They received messages from God and saw visions.[20] The actual power of performing miraculous acts was limited, however, to the apostles and those who had received the laying on of the apostles' hands.

Laying On Hands

The "laying on of hands" indicates different things according to the context in which it occurs in the New Testament.

The laying on of hands was connected with the healing of the sick. In the Gospel of Mark it is used six times in connection with healings.[21] Of particular significance is Mark's account of the great commission. Laying hands on the sick to heal was one of the confirming signs.

> *And these signs will accompany those who have believed:*
> *In My name they will cast out demons, they will speak with*
> *new tongues; they will pick up serpents, and if they drink*
> *any deadly poison, it shall not hurt them; they will lay hands*
> *on the sick, and they will recover.*[22]

The Acts narrative also contains two references to the laying on of hands in working miracles of healing.[23]

The laying on of hands is also connected with giving sanction or authority to another. It is used in this sense with reference to the six men appointed by the apostles to look after the Grecian widows.[24] The church at Antioch "laid hands" on Barnabas and Saul when they began their first journey.[25] Timothy received the laying on of the elders' hands when he was sent by the church at Lystra to accompany Paul.[26]

The "laying on of hands" was connected with blessing. This use of the laying on of hands goes back to Jacob blessing the children of Joseph.[27] Jesus blessed little children and laid His hands on them.

> *And He took them in His arms and began blessing them, laying*
> *His hands upon them.*[28]

As already shown, Luke makes special reference to the "laying on of apostles' hands". That there is something unique about it is shown in the account of the Samaritans' receiving the Holy Spirit.[29]

Simon observed that individuals could receive the Holy Spirit in a way they had not received Him at baptism. This was made possible through the apostles, Peter and John, laying hands on the person and praying. After seeing the cause and effect of this, he wanted to obtain this power to bestow the Holy Spirit by the laying on of his own hands. The rebuke which Peter gave to him should be sufficient to warn men of all time not to covet miraculous powers which were not meant for them.

> . . .*May your silver perish with you, because you thought you could obtain the gift of God with money. ' You have no part or portion in this matter, for your heart is not right before God. Therefore repent of this wickedness of yours . . .*[30]

This unique power received by those upon whom the apostles laid hands can be observed in other places. Stephen and Philip were two of the seven who received the "laying on the apostles' hands".[31] Both of them were later to be seen working miracles.[32] The twelve men at Ephesus whom Paul baptized were able to speak with other tongues and prophesy, but it was after Paul had laid his hands on them. Timothy is reminded of the gift of God which he received by the laying on of Paul's hands.[33]

In a secondary way one is able to see the significance of an apostle visiting a church in the first century. At Corinth Paul indicates that they were not "lacking in any gift".[34] Later on in the epistle Paul lists fourteen spiritual gifts most of which are miraculous in their nature. Paul had been at Corinth for an extended period and had ample opportunity to "lay hands" on numerous individuals.

At Rome it was a different story. Paul wrote that he wanted to come to them so he could impart spiritual gifts.[35] They must have lacked such gifts or he would not have had this desire. Later in the Roman epistle Paul lists certain spiritual gifts that the church there possessed.[36] It is significant that the spiritual gifts listed in Romans are not necessarily miraculous in their nature.

Could it be that the difference in the spiritual gifts at Corinth and Rome was due to the fact that there is no record of an apostle being in Rome before Paul wrote Romans? Without the presence of an apostle, there would be no miraculous powers bestowed through the laying on of their hands.

It should be observed that there is no incident in the New Testament in which there were such powers transmitted by any one except apostles. It is true that Paul speaks of gifts given to Timothy with the laying on of the hands of the presbytery.[37] Some would suggest that this means the hands of the presbytery was the means by which Timothy obtained spiritual gifts. Timothy received such a spiritual gift through (*dia*) the laying on of Paul's hands.[38] A different preposition is used in connection with the laying on the the hands of the presbytery. It is "with" (*meta*). The gift Timothy possessed came "through" the laying on of Paul's hands and "with" the laying on of the hands of the presbytery. Perhaps when Timothy was sent out by the church in Lystra, Paul laid hands on him to give him the spiritual gift. At the same time the presbytery laid hands on him to show their sanction.

Luke emphasizes the power connected with the apostles. Just the shadow of Peter was enough to heal.[39] Handkerchicfs and aprons from Paul was enough to work miracles.[40] The apostolic office is emphasized by Luke in recording the miracles of Acts.

Confirming Signs

Luke intended that miracles would be a confirmation that the man and message were from God.

This was one of the points Peter made in his sermon on the Day of Pentecost to prove that Jesus had been raised. The people had just witnessed four miracles. Peter tells them the source of these miracles and their purpose.

> *This Jesus God raised up again to which we are all witnesses. Therefore having been exalted to the right hand of God, and having received from the Father the promise of the Holy Spirit, He has poured forth this which you both see and hear.[41]*

Peter used the miracle of healing the lame man at the gate called Beautiful as a confirming sign that God had raised Jesus from the dead.

> *But you disowned the Holy and Righteous One, and asked for a murderer to be granted to you, but put to death the Prince of life, the one whom God raised from the dead, -- a fact to which we are witnesses. And on the basis of faith in His name, it is the name of Jesus which has strengthened this man whom you see and know.[42]*

In the miracles of judgment God punished those who resisted His will. There was also in these miracles the purpose of confirmation. The authority of the apostles was confirmed when Ananias and Sapphira were struck dead.[43] The Divine sanction of the church is to be seen by the miracle of Herod being eaten with worms. God did not allow Herod's persecution of the church or his arrogant pride to go unpunished.[44] God confirmed the power and the authority of Paul by striking Elymas blind.[45]

Paul used the fact that signs and wonders had been done among the Gentiles to show that God approved of the Gospel being taken to them.[46]

Peter used the miracle of speaking in tongues at Cornelius' house as evidence to show the brethren in Judea that "God has granted to the Gentiles also, the repentance that leads to life".[47]

In a secondary way miracles in Acts seemed to be for building confidence within the church. Not only did the miracles confirm to others God's sanction of the apostles, but they also confirmed to the apostles themselves that God was with them. The miracles gave them boldness.

We cannot stop speaking what we have seen and heard.[48]

The miracles and signs that Peter had seen and heard were the basis for his boldness. After the apostles were released from prison and went back to their own company, they prayed for confidence and a sign from God.[49] Their meeting place was shaken, and they were filled with the Holy Spirit and spoke the word of God with "boldness".[50]

The text does not state "confidence" as a purpose for miracles. It is clear, however, that miracles resulted in greater boldness within the New Testament church.

Wonders --- True and False

Luke, throughout the Acts narrative, brings into contrast the apostolic miracles and those claimed by magicians, sorcerers and exorcists.

Simon the Magician in Samaria made great claims for himself and was called the "Great Power of God" by the people who saw his magic art.[51] The message and the miracles of Philip were so great that even Simon was converted. He was amazed at the signs and wonders performed by Philip. It is not merely incidental to the story that Simon desired to buy the power to lay hands on people that they might receive the Holy Spirit. The connection of miraculous claims and money is not new. Peter forever divorces the two by his response to Simon.

> *But Peter said to him, 'May your silver perish with you, because you thought you could obtain the gift of God with money! You have no part or portion in this matter, for your heart is not right before God.[52]*

Another statement of Peter which disassociates miracles and money is connected with the healing of the lame man. He said, "I do not possess silver and gold, but what I do have I give to you". [53]

Elymas Bar-Jesus was a magician and false prophet which Barnabas and Saul confronted at Paphos.[54] As was often the case in the Graeco-Roman culture, the proconsul Sergius Paulus had such a man for an advisor. Elymas opposed Barnabas and Saul and sought to turn Sergius Paulus away from the faith. Paul struck him blind for this opposition. This miracle caused the proconsul to believe. Luke seemed to be showing that the power of God and the message of the Gospel were greater and stronger than mighty magicians.

Luke tells of some traveling Jewish exorcists at Ephesus.[55] They were identified as the seven sons of Sceva, a Jewish chief priest.

Exorcism was very common in the first century. Jesus mentioned that there were Jews who cast out demons.[56] Exorcism formulae are common in the ancient papyri which have been discovered in the Near East.[57] Jesus and His disciples cast out demons as a part of their miraculous signs.

These exorcists had no doubt heard about Paul casting out demons in the name of Jesus. They tried to do the same thing. The response of the demon was to attack them and drive them out of the house wounded and naked. The demons said, "I recognize Jesus and I know about Paul, but who are you?".[58] These exorcists had attempted to counterfeit the miracles of Paul. They thought saying the right words and using the right name would enable them to perform miracles. The power of God is not a magic formula of words. The purpose of casting out demons was not just to release a man from being possessed. It was to show the sanction of God upon certain men and their message.

Luke records Paul's confrontation with a fortune teller at Philippi.[59] The fortune teller was a woman slave who was possessed by a demon. She made her masters a lot of money by telling fortunes. Paul cast the demon out of her and this angered her masters. Their hope of profit was gone. They accused Paul and Silas before the magistrates and had them put in prison.

The connection of claiming to know the future and making profit is still a part of today's religious world. Just as the woman fortune teller at Philippi spoke some truth and gave sanction to Paul and Silas as being servants of the most high God, some contemporary religionists speak some truth and claim allegiance to Jesus Christ. Paul refused to give sanction to the woman. He would not compromise the faith in Jesus Christ with other beliefs in the name of tolerance. He would not associate with anyone who was basically in error just because she or he taught some truth.

One of the most graphic examples of repentance in the New Testament is found in connection with the people in Ephesus who had practiced the magic arts before they became Christians. Luke records it thus:

> *Many also of those who had believed kept coming, confessing*
> *and disclosing their practices. And many of those who*
> *practiced magic brought their books together and began*
> *burning them in the sight of all; and they counted up the*
> *price of them and found it fifty thousand pieces of silver.[60]*

A bonfire of books worth approximately $1,160,000 by current monetary standards is a monumental expression of repentance. When the Ephesians became Christians, they wanted to divorce themselves from magic, the occult and all other things which would tempt them to compromise their faith.

A Christian cannot be divided in his loyalties. He cannot be half Christian and half a part of the occult. He cannot be a faithful disciple of Jesus and flirt with false religious practices at the same time. Christianity is totally incompatible with contemporary claims of exorcism, astrology, occult rituals, miracles, healings, tongue speaking and latter day revelations. Like the pagan wonder workers of the first century, such who claim to practice these today make big claims. Like the pagan wonder workers of the first century, their signs are false and their teaching is error.

Three things should be remembered about the miracles in Acts. First, they were worked by either the apostles or those who had the opportunity of receiving the laying on the the apostles' hands. Second, their purpose was to confirm the man and message as being from God. Third, the genuine miracles worked by God are not be be confused or compromised with the false claims of men.

ENDNOTES

[1] Acts 2:1-6

[2] Acts 5:12

[3] Acts 9:11-12; 19:12

[4] Acts 8:6-8; 19:6

[5] Acts 5:12

[6] Acts 5:1-10

[7] Acts 5:13

[8] Acts 6:8; 8:6-8, 13; 9:12-17

[9] Acts 6:6

[10] Acts 1:8; 2:1-4

[11] II Corinthians 12:12

[12] John 20:22

[13] Ephesians 4:8-11

[14] Hebrews 3:1

[15] Hebrews 3:2

[16] I Corinthians 9:1-6

[17] Acts 11:15-17

[18] Acts 8:14-18

[19] Acts 10:3

[20] Acts 9:12; 11:20; 21:10-12

[21] Acts 5:23; 6:2, 5; 7:32; 8:23; 16:18

[22] Mark 16:17-18

[23] Acts 9:12, 17; 28:8

[24] Acts 6:6

[25] Acts 13:3

[26] I Timothy 4:14 and Acts 16:1

[27] Genesis 48:8-19

[28] Mark 10:16

[29] Acts 8:18-19

[30] Acts 8:19-22

[31] Acts 6:6

[32] Acts 6:8; 8:6-8, 13

[33] I Timothy 1:6

[34] I Corinthians 1:7

[35] Romans 1:11

[36] Romans 12:6-8

[37] I Timothy 4:14

[38] II Timothy 1:6

[39] Acts 5:15-16

[40] Acts 15:12

[41] Acts 2:32-33

[42] Acts 3:14-16

[43] Acts 5:11-13

[44] Acts 12:1-23

[45] Acts 13:7-12

[46]Acts 15:12

[47]Acts 11:14-18

[48]Acts 4:20

[49]Acts 4:29-30

[50]Acts 4:31

[51]Acts 8:9-11

[52]Acts 3:20-21

[53]Acts 3:6

[54]Acts 13:6-12

[55]Acts 19:13-17

[56]Luke 11:19

[57]See page 91

[58]Acts 19:15

[59]Acts 16:16-19

[60]Acts 19:18-19

CHAPTER 6

MIRACLES IN
THE EPISTLES

Miracles are not explicit in the epistles. There is no walking on water, healing the sick or raising the dead. This does not mean that the miraculous is absent. The chart on the Miracles in the Epistles shows four general references and numerous passages related to miraculous spiritual gifts.

It should be observed again that there is a decline in the miraculous events from the Gospels to Acts and from Acts to the Epistles. There was also a decline in miracles from the early epistles to the latter epistles. The Corinthian correspondence has much more of the miraculous in it than do the Pastoral Epistles.

There were also other changes which paralleled this decline. There seemed to be a change in the purpose of the miraculous from that of confirmation of the man and message to that of edification of the church. The Gospels and Acts clearly show confirmation as the basic purpose. The epistles focus on the exercise of miraculous spiritual gifts for the benefit of the whole church.[1] Just as the nature of the miraculous changed, the purpose of the miraculous changed. The change was from that of wonder working for confirmation to that of the exercise of spiritual gifts for the common good. It was from confirmation to edification.

There appear to be no miracles in the epistles which conform to the nature of the miracles in the Gospels and Acts. This may be due to one or a combination of the following reasons.

First, the decline could have been because there was not a need for miracles of the explicit nature. The person of Jesus had been fully confirmed by His miracles.[2] The message of the apostles had been fully confirmed by their miracles. There was no new Christ nor was there any new Gospel. Therefore the confirming miracles were no longer needed.

Second,the purpose of the epistles was to instruct Christians in doctrinal, ethical, moral and practical implications of being a disciple of Jesus Christ. They did not need signs to believe. They already believed. The epistles sought to motivate the readers to be true and faithful to what they already believed. The purpose of the epistles therefore would nullify the need of the miraculous.

The literary style of the epistles is that of practical hortatory letters and doctrinal tracts. The literary style of the Gospels is that of a historical narrative. The literary style of Acts is that of a travelogue laced with polemic sermons. Miracles fit into the style of the latter groups more than the first.

Miracles in the Epistles:

I. General References (5)

Romans 15:19	Galatians 3:5
II Corinthians 12:2	Hebrews 2:4

II. Spiritual Gifts

Romans 1:11; 12:6-8	Grace Gifts at Rome
I Corinthians 1:5-7;	
12:1-14:40	Grace Gifts at Corinth
Ephesians 4:7-16	Grace Gifts at Ephesus
I Timothy 4:14	
II Timothy 1:6	Grace Gifts to Timothy
I Peter 4:10	Grace Gifts as Stewardship

III. False Signs (11)

Matthew 2:24
Mark 13:22   False Prophets and False Signs
II Corinthians
    11:13-15   Deceitful Workers
Galatians 1:6-9   Teaching Another Gospel
Colossians 2:18-19   False Teachers Claiming Visions
II Thessalonians
    2:8-12   Signs to Deceive, No Love of Truth
I Timothy 4:1-3   Deceitful Spirits Teaching False
II Timothy 3:13   Imposters Who Deceive
Titus 3:13   Men Who Deceive for Gain
Revelation 13:11-14 Beast Deceive Men with Signs
Revelations 16:12-16 Unclean Spirits Perform Signs
Revelations 19:19-20 False Prophet Deceives with Signs

The four passages in the epistles which make a general reference to miracles reveal two things.

First, there is no need of recording the specific miracles since the readers already knew about them and understood their importance. In Galatians, Paul uses the presence of miracles among them to show the priority of faith over the works of the law.

> *Does He then who provides you with the Spirit and works miracles among you, do it by the works of the Law, or by the hearing with faith?*[3]

Miracles were an acknowledged fact in the churches. There was no need to give specifics.

Second, the confirming nature of miracles is still understood as being their basic purpose. Paul argues for the validity of his apostleship by referring to the signs, wonders and miracles he had done in their midst.[4] He calls them the "signs of an apostle".

Perhaps the clearest expression of this point is to be found in Hebrews. After warning not to neglect so great salvation, he reminds them that it had come first from the Lord, then from those who heard the Lord and finally to the recipients of the book of Hebrews. Not only were there the witnesses of those who heard the Lord, but there was also the witness from God in the form of signs, wonders and miracles.

> *. . . How shall we escape if we neglect so great a salvation?*
> *After it was at the first spoken through the Lord, it was*
> *confirmed to us by those who heard, God also bearing witness*
> *with them, both by signs and wonders and by various*
> *miracles. . .5*

Though there are no incidents of miracles recorded in the epistles, they are acknowledged as having taken place for the purpose of confirming God sanctioned men and a God sanctioned message.

Spiritual Gifts

The miraculous element in the epistles focuses on the exercise of spiritual gifts distributed among different members of the body. They were to be used for the common good. A number of passages reflect this.

> *But to each one is given the manifestation of the Spirit*
> *for the common good.6*

> *And He gave some as apostles, and some as prophets, and*
> *some as evangelists, and some as pastors and teachers, for*
> *the equipping of the saints for the work of service, to the*
> *building up of the body of Christ.7*

> *As since we have gifts that differ according to the grace*
> *given to us, let each exercise them accordingly; if*
> *prophesying, according to the proportion of his faith; if*
> *service, in his serving; or he who teaches, in his*
> *teaching; or he who exhorts, in his exhortation; he*
> *who gives, with liberality; he who leads, with diligence;*
> *he who shows mercy, with cheerfulness.8*

> *As each one has received a special gift, employ it in serving*
> *one another, as good stewards of the manifold grace of God.9*

66

At Corinth, Paul says there were different gifts and ministries but only one Spirit. Each one should therefore use his gift for the common good.

To the church at Ephesus, Paul explains that "to each one of us grace was given according to the measure of Christ's gift".[10] These grace gifts were to be used for uniting and building up the whole body.[11]

The same focus is to be found in the letter to the Romans. There are many members but one body. Members do not have the same gifts or the same functions. Each member, however, is connected to the other, and all are to exercise their gifts for the good of the whole.[12]

Peter expresses a similar teaching. There are diversities of gifts in the body, but each one is to be used for the good of the whole. Those who possess the gifts do not own them. They are only stewards of the grace gifts of God.[13]

Two lists of spiritual gifts are given in I Corinthians.[14] These lists contain fourteen different gifts, all of which may be miraculous. Some of the gifts like knowledge, wisdom, tongues, interpretation of tongues and teaching can be naturally acquired gifts. They can become miraculous gifts when given by God without the natural process of training or study. Other gifts like healing, miracles and the distinguishing of spirits are miraculous in their nature. They could be obtained only by a direct act of God. The context would suggest that all fourteen of the gifts listed were miraculous

Another list of spiritual gifts is given in Romans.[15] This list contains seven items, none of which are miraculous in their nature. There is nothing in the context which would suggest that they were miraculous. Paul wanted to come to Rome that he might impart some spiritual gifts to them.[16] Such a desire would seem odd if they already possessed miraculous spiritual gifts which came through the laying on of apostles' hands. There is no evidence of an apostle being in Rome before the book of Romans was written. This context would suggest that the spiritual gifts in Romans were non-miraculous in their nature.

The word most often used for spiritual gifts is *charisma*. It literally means "grace gift". The word is used for both natural and supernatural gifts. It would be a mistake to identify every gift for which this term is used as miraculous. The emphasis of the word is on the grace through which the gift comes. It refers to gifts that were not earned.

This could mean natural gifts with which God has endowed an individual. This could mean supernatural gifts which were obtained through the laying on of apostles' hands. Natural gifts might be the case in Romans. Supernatural gifts might be the case in I Corinthians.

One may divide the New Testament miracles into four phases. Phase one would be the miracles which were worked by Jesus. Phase two would be the miracles worked by the apostles and the seventy. Phase three would be the miracles worked by those who received the laying on of the apostles' hands. Phase four would be miracles accepted in faith by those who received the testimony of those who witnessed the other three phases.

Each of the phases was different. Phase one focused on the person of Jesus. Phase two focused on the name of Jesus by which miracles were done. Phase three focused on the exercise of spiritual gifts. Phase four focuses on the Scriptures which reveal the miracles and by which one comes to believe.   It was of this last phase that Jesus said, "Blessed are they who did not see, and yet believed".[17]

Each of these phases had a primary period of time. Phase one is reflected in the Gospels. Phase two is reflected in Acts. Phase three is reflected in the epistles. The final phase will last till Jesus comes.

Each of the first three phases has ceased. Phase one ceased when Jesus ascended to heaven. Phase two ceased when the apostles and the seventy died. Phase three ceased when the last person who received the laying on of apostles' hands died.

The passing away of phase three was predicted in the Scriptures. Paul told the Corinthians in the context of discussing miraculous spiritual gifts that such gifts would pass.

> *Love never fails; but if there are gifts of prophecy, they will be done away; if there are tongues, they will cease; if there is knowledge, it will be done away. For we know in part, and we prophesy in part; but when the perfect comes, the partial will be done away.[18]*

The temporary nature of these spiritual gifts is clearly stated. Prophecy and knowledge would pass away and tongues would cease of themselves.[19]

Paul also wrote to the Ephesians about the temporary nature of the spiritual gifts.

And He gave some as apostles, and some as prophets, and some as evangelists, and some as pastors and teachers, for the equipping of the saints for the work of service, to the building up of the body of Christ; until we all attain to the unity of the faith, and of the knowledge of the Son of God, to a mature man, to the measure of the stature which belongs to the fullness of Christ.[20]

The gifts referred to here are different gifts of leadership; some of which were connected with miraculous power and confined to the apostolic age. All of the gifts could have been miraculous since Paul, an apostle, had spent more than three years in Ephesus. In discussing the gifts, he limits their duration. They would exist "until" three things happened: First, they would endure "until" we attain the unity of the faith. Second, they were to endure "until" we attain to the knowledge of the Son of God. Third, they were to endure "until" we attain to the measure of the stature which belongs to Christ. It is not the purpose in this study to determine when this was to take place from this passage, but only to establish that it was to happen.

Abuse of Spiritual Gifts

Most of the information that the New Testament gives concerning spiritual gifts comes from Paul's refutation of their abuse.[21] It should be observed that the exercise of the spiritual gifts at Corinth was not an approved pattern. They were being abused.

In chapter twelve, Paul begins his response to the abuse of gifts by telling the Corinthian Christians that they were acting like pagans.

You know that when you were pagans, you were led astray to dumb idols, however you were lead.[22]

Just as pagans in the Dionysian cult would drug their minds by drinking wine to lose their reason during their cultic worship, the Corinthian Christians were divorcing reason from the exercise of their spiritual gifts.[23]

Like those engaged in Dionysian cult-worship, Christians were becoming drunk during the observance of the Lord's Supper.[24]

Just as the Eleusinian cult would become "beside themselves" in the ecstasy of their rituals, the Corinthians Christians were conducting confused and irrational worship in their assemblies. Everyone would talk at once with no concern for being understood. If no one understood, no one could be edified.[25] Such activities were like the pagans and must be stopped.

Just as the Greek mystery religions would encourage their devotees to give forth ecstatic utterances as being evidence that the gods were in them, the Corinthians were abusing the gift of speaking in other languages by not caring if it were understood.[26] Irrational speaking was not to be tolerated in the assemblies of the church.[27]

In chapter thirteen, Paul shows that the miraculous spiritual gifts were passing away. In getting so wrapped up in the showiness of speaking in other languages --- which would cease --- the Corinthians were neglecting unselfish love. The most glamorous miraculous gifts are nothing without love, he argues.[28]

In chapter fourteen, Paul corrects the abuse of miraculous gifts which were causing confusion in the assembles. The Corinthians had become so engrossed in the externals of the miraculous gifts that they had forgotten their purpose of edification. Paul exhorts that prayer and praise must be understood by the one who gives it[29],and the one who hears it.[30]

The abuse of miraculous spiritual gifts happened at Corinth after the need for them began to decline. Those were soon to pass away. With their passing should have gone the temptation to make miraculous desires the substance of one's Christian commitment.

False Signs

The chart of Miracles in the Epistles lists eleven passages in which the New Testament warns of deceitful wonder workers and false signs. It should be observed that any time the epistles speak of signs in the latter times, it refers to false signs from false prophets.

Jesus warned that false prophets with great signs would lead many astray.[31] He said not to believe them. The apostle John warns against believing just anybody who claims to have the Spirit of God.

> *Beloved, do not believe every spirit, but test the spirits*
> *to see whether they are from God; because many false*
> *prophets have gone out into the world.[32]*

There are unholy spirits just as there is the Holy Spirit. One must not allow a false prophet to counterfeit the holy with the profane.

Some characteristics of these false prophets who work signs are shown in the Scriptures. First, they disguise themselves as apostles of Christ.[33] Second, they preach another Gospel.[34] Third, they work false wonders.[35] Fourth, they deceive for gain.[36] Fifth, they teach false doctrine.[37] Sixth, they claim to have visions.[38]

In Revelation, signs are worked by the beast, unclean spirits like frogs and the false prophet. All of these work in opposition to God and Christ. The ultimate end of these false sign workers is the lake of fire.[39]

Jesus himself predicted that there would be those who claimed to follow Him and claim to do mighty works in His name. He refused to acknowledge them as His disciples.

> *Many will say to Me on that day, Lord, Lord, did we not*
> *prophesy in Your name, and in Your name cast out demons,*
> *and in Your name perform many miracles? And then I will*
> *declare to them, I never knew you; **Depart from me, you***
> ***who practice lawlessness.**[40]*

What Jesus predicted took place in the first century and has continued to take place in every generation since. Contemporary claims of the miraculous are not new. Contemporary claims of the miraculous are not different from pagan claims. Contemporary claims of the miraculous are counterfeits and cannot be proven.

For these reasons one should not give passive tolerance to such claims or excuse them as merely being pious fantasies. It is wrong to claim the name of Christ as the authority for psychosomatic cures or paranormal happenings. Contemporary frauds claiming to be miracles nullify the genuine miracles of the New Testament in the minds of the people who witness them.

It is not a sign of weak faith to question the miraculous claims of contemporary religion; it is a sign of mature faith. The New Testament warnings about false prophets and lying wonders must be heeded today.

Sickness Not Healed

No study of the miraculous healings in the epistles would be complete without consideration of those incidents in which the apostles and their companions were not healed of sicknesses. This phenomenon occurs many times.

Trophimus was left at Miletus by Paul because he was sick.[41]

Timothy was instructed to use a little wine for his stomach's sake because he had frequent ailments.[42]

Paul was sick when he preached to the Galatians. His sickness did not cause the Galatians to think any less of his authority or message.

> *But you know that it was because of a bodily illness that I preached the gospel to you the first time; and that which was a trial to you in my bodily condition you did not despise or loathe, but you received me as an angel of God, as Christ Jesus Himself.[43]*

Paul was also plagued with a thorn in the flesh which God refused to remove. Paul prayed for its removal three times, but God did not heal him.[44]

Epaphroditus, the messenger of the Phillipian church, was sick "to the point of death".[45] Paul did not heal him with a miracle.

These incidents of non-healing pose a problem. Why were these individuals not healed? They were connected to the apostles who healed others. Some were in churches where there were individuals with the "gift of healing".[46] Certainly they were in the company of elders who could anoint them with oil and pray for them.[47] It is impossible to know all that was involved in these non-healings, but the following three suggestions might help in understanding,

First, a unique factor of the New Testament miracles is that they were unselfish. Jesus did not turn stones into bread when he had fasted for forty days, but He provided enough bread for two multitudes when they were hungry. Jesus refused to destroy a Samaritan village because they refused to receive Him, but He cast money changers out of the temple because they defiled the house of God. Jesus refused to call a legion of angels to defend Himself, but He restored the ear of Malchus that was cut off by Peter. Miracles were not performed for ease, comfort or convenience of the ones who worked them. They were worked for the benefit of others.

Second, a unique factor about New Testament miracles is that they had as their purpose confirmation. They were not worked at random. They were not the result of sentimental compassion. They were not worked to satisfy the desires of the curiosity seekers. They were to confirm either the man or the message as being from God. If the incident of non-healing were such that no confirmation was needed, then to work a miracle would be without purpose. If the purpose of the miraculous were merely to heal the sick, why was not all Palestine healed in Jesus' day? The Devil tried to get Jesus to perform miracles for selfish purposes. Jesus' response was, "Thou shalt not tempt the Lord, thy God".[48]

Third, a significant factor about the non-healings in the New Testament is that they all happened near the close of the apostolic period.

The one exception is the inability of the apostles to heal the epileptic demoniac boy.[49] In this case the apostles could not heal because of their lack of faith.[50] Jesus did heal him at once. This one incident does not break the pattern of the non-healing incidents coming at the close of the apostolic ministry. This incident was caused by a faith deficiency in the apostles. This is not the case of the other non-healings.

It has already been shown that incidents of miracles declined from the beginning to the end of the apostolic period. There was less and less a need of confirmation as the faith was established and the Gospel message was confirmed in the life of the church. The non-healing incidents serve to establish the fact that the purpose of miracles was confirmation. It would only be natural for most of the non-healings to be near the end of the apostolic period.

ENDNOTES

[1]See page 15, 19-20

[2]John 20:30-31

[3]Galatians 3:5

[4]II Corinthians 12:12

[5]Hebrews 2:3-4

[6]I Corinthians 12:7

[7]Ephesians 4:11-12

[8]Romans 12:6-8

[9]I Peter 4:10

[10]Ephesians 4:7

[11]Ephesians 4:12

[12]Romans 12:4-8

[13]I Peter 4:1-12

[14]I Corinthians 12:8-10, 28-30

[15]Romans 12:6-8

[16]Romans 1:11

[17]John 20:29

[18]I Corinthians 13:8-10

[19]See Jimmy Jividen, *Glossolalia* (Fort Worth: Star Bible Publications, 1971) pp. 144-147

[20]Ephesians 4:11-13

[21]I Corinthians 12-14

[22]I Corinthians 12:12

[23]I Corinthians 14:14-16

[24]I Corinthians 11:21

[25]I Corinthians 14:26

[26]See Jimmy Jividen, *op. cit.*, pp. 107-142

[27]I Corinthians 14:28

[28] I Corinthians 13:1-3

[29] I Corinthians 14:14-15

[30] I Corinthians 14:16, 26

[31] Matthew 24:24

[32] I John 4:1

[33] II Corinthians 12:13-15

[34] Galatians 1:6-8

[35] II Thessalonians 2:9

[36] Titus 1:10

[37] I Timothy 4:1-3

[38] Colossians 2:18-19

[39] Revelation 19:19-20

[40] Matthew 7:22-23

[41] II Timothy 4:20

[42] I Timothy 5:23

[43] Galatians 4:13-14

[44] II Corinthians 12:7-10

[45] Philippians 2:25-30

[46] I Corinthians 12:9

[47] James 5:13-18

[48] Matthew 4:7

[49] Matthew 17:15-18

[50] Matthew 17:19-21

Miracles: From God or Man?

CHAPTER 7

PURPOSES OF MIRACLES

If one is able to understand the purposes of the New Testament miracles as expressed by Jesus and the New Testament authors, much of the confusion over the miraculous would be cleared up. One would be able to know what a miracle was and be able to distinguish between a true and false miracle. One would understand why the occurrence of the miraculous is not static throughout history but changes from one period to another.

A discussion of the purposes of miracles as they were used by the different New Testament writers has already been given.[1] By drawing this material together, one is able to discern that there are two basic purposes of the New Testament miracles and three secondary purposes.

Halley's Handbook gives the purpose of Jesus' miracles in this statement:

> *Jesus' miracles imply an exercise of creative power. They were a part of God's way of authenticating Jesus' mission. Jesus said that if He had not done works that no other ever did, they would not have had sin (John 15:24), thus indicating that He regarded His miracles as proofs that He was from God. Then, too, His miracles were the natural expression of His sympathy for suffering humanity.*[2]

This statement gives one of the basic purposes of miracles as perceived by this author and one of the secondary uses. A study of several New Testament passages should expand this statement of the purpose of miracles.

Proof of Claim

A basic purpose of the New Testament miracles both in the work of Jesus and His disciples was confirmation. They were used as proof that the claims they made were from God. They were used to show sanction of their message.

This is clearly expressed in the summary statement of John's Gospel.

> *Many other signs therefore Jesus also performed in the presence of the disciples, which are not written in this book; but these have been written that you may believe that Jesus is the Christ the Son of God;[3]*

John had already recorded the statement which Nicodemus made to Jesus, that "no one can do these signs that You do unless God is with him".[4] Even John's use of the word "sign" for a miraculous event reflects this purpose. Signs point to something beyond themselves. Jesus' signs pointed to His being who He claimed to be, the Son of God. Signs were to produce faith in Jesus and His message.

The confirming nature of miracles is clearly stated in the closing verses of Mark. Jesus' statement to His apostles after giving the great commission was this:

> *And these signs will accompany those who have believed; in My name they will cast out demons, they will speak with new tongues; they will pick up serpents, and if they drink any deadly poison, it shall not hurt them; they will lay hands on the sick, and they will recover. So then, when the Lord Jesus had spoken to them, He was received up into the heaven, and sat down at the right hand of God. And they went out and preached everywhere, while the Lord worked with them, and confirmed the word by the signs that followed.[5]*

The promise of miracles accompanying believers is stated in the first part of the passage. The fact that this did happen is stated in the last part of the passage. The same root word, *akoloutheo* meaning "to follow", is used at the beginning and at the end of the passage. Signs will "accompany" those who have believed. The word was confirmed by the signs that "followed". It is clear that Mark understood the statement of Jesus to mean that these miraculous signs were for the purpose of confirming the word which was preached.

It should be noted that the promise was not that all believers would work signs, but that signs would accompany believers. It is quite evident that all believers did not work all of the signs even in New Testament times.[6] The promise was --- and the reality is --- that signs do accompany all believers in all places and at all times but not always in the same way.

First, signs accompanied the believers in fact. The apostles and their company worked signs when they preached. These signs confirmed their words.

Second, signs accompanied the believers through testimony. Those who saw the miracles of Jesus and witnessed the apostolic signs could bear witness to what they saw. The message that they heard was confirmed by signs, wonders and miracles. Those who first heard the message and saw the signs could confirm it to others.[7]

Third, signs accompanied believers through the witness of the Scriptures. A record of some of the miracles performed by Jesus and the apostles is given in the New Testament. Wherever the New Testament has gone , the miracles which are recorded in it go also. Signs accompany the believers through the inspired Scriptures. John said, "these things are written that you might believe".[8]

It is a mistake to interpret this passage as a promise that all believers would work miracles or that miracles will be worked for all time. The promise is only that " signs will accompany those who have believed".

It should be observed that the five signs specifically mentioned in the passage ---casting out demons, speaking with new tongues, picking up serpents, drinking deadly poison without harm and laying hands on the sick so that they will be healed --- are all supernatural or miraculous in their nature. That is, it takes the direct intervention of God to alter the course of nature for them to happen. Three of these signs have often been counterfeited by men throughout the centuries.

People claim to cast out demons, but there is no objective evidence to indicate that such really happens. They can only offer their subjective testimony. Heretics, witch doctors and spiritualists do the same thing.

People claim to speak in tongues, but the ecstatic utterances they give are not the foreign languages of men but gibberish. Heretics, pagans and spiritualists do the same thing. The New Testament gift of tongues was languages of men which men could speak without having studied. This gift was miraculously acquired.[9]

People claim to heal the sick, but only certain ones with specific kinds of illnesses. The healing claims are not objectively substantiated as being supernatural or miraculous. They are no more than therapy for psycosomatic illnesses and religious explanations of paranormal events. They are made to seem so marvelous because of the exaggerated testimony which is given in emotional surroundings. Heretics, pagans and spiritualists do the same thing.

Rarely do men try to counterfeit the signs of drinking deadly poison or picking up snakes. When they do, they become sick and often die. Newspapers have often recorded the deaths of individuals involved in the "snake handling cults" who use this passage to justify their ritual. Jim Jones and his followers are contemporary testimonies to the fact that drinking deadly poison --- even if it is done in religious ritual --- can be fatal.

The confirming nature of miracles is expressed in the sermon Peter preached on the day of Pentecost. One of the proofs Peter gave for the resurrection and Lordship of Jesus was the miracles which the multitude saw.[10]

The multitude could see the miracle of cloven tongues like as fire sitting on the apostles. They could hear the sound as of a rushing wind that accompanied the coming of the Holy Spirit. They could hear the apostles speaking in languages which they had not studied. Miracles were happening and Peter said that they confirmed the person, the message and the promise of Jesus.

The confirming nature of Jesus' signs is given by His own testimony. He healed the paralytic to show that He had the authority and the approval of God to forgive sins.

> *But in order that you may know that the Son of Man has*
> *authority on earth to forgive sins --- He said to the paralytic,*
> *'I say to you, rise, take up your pallet and go home'. And he*
> *rose and immediately took up the pallet and went out in*
> *the sight of all; so that they were all amazed and were*

> *glorifying God, saying, 'We have never seen anything like this'.[11]*

What Jesus said was confirmed by the things He did. That was the purpose for His mighty works.

Miracles were Jesus' proof of claim. One might say that miracles were a theological necessity if God wanted to give man a new revelation. The history of God dealing with man in the Scriptures shows that miracles always accompanied new revelations that God gave to man.

Fulfillment of Scriptures

The second major purpose of miracles is that they serve to fulfill the Messianic prophecies of the Old Testament Scriptures. When Moses came, he worked miracles. When Elijah and Elisha came, they worked miracles. When the Messiah would come and "declare all things to us"[12], He would work miracles.

This purpose of miracles is prominent in Matthew. He often used a fulfillment formula before quoting Old Testament Scriptures. He then would apply them to Jesus as the fulfillment of the coming Messiah.

When John the Baptist was in prison, he sent some of his disciples to see Jesus. He wanted to know if He were the Messiah or should they look for another. Jesus did not answer the question directly, but told them to relate to John His mighty miracles.[13] This was enough to show John that He was the Messiah. The Messiah was to do the miracles which Jesus was doing.

Jesus came back to Nazareth early in His ministry and went into the synagogue on the Sabbath day.[14] He was given the Scroll of the Scriptures to read. He chose Isaiah 61:1-2. He knew this to be a Messianic prediction which was being fulfilled in His ministry. It dealt with the Messiah working wonders. He would heal the blind, free the captive and preach the Gospel to the poor. Such was Jesus' ministry. Jesus said, "Today this Scripture has been fulfilled in your hearing".

The Jews of Jesus' day understood that the Messiah was to be a miracle worker. One of the reasons that people believed in Jesus was that he fulfilled the expectations which they had of the coming Messiah.

> *But many of the multitude believed in Him; and they were*
> *saying, 'When the Christ shall come, He will not perform*
> *more signs than those which this man has, will He?'*[15]

The Old Testament prediction of a wonder working Messiah was fulfilled in Jesus. One might say that miracles were a theological necessity to confirm Jesus' Messiahship.

Secondary Purposes of Miracles

Aside from the primary purposes of miracles as stated above, there are three secondary uses in the New Testament. A secondard purpose would be some consequence of a miracle which is not stated as a purpose in the Biblical text itself, but is evident from the circumstances which surround the event

First, miracles are a reflection of Jesus' compassion. On at least six occasions in the Gospels, it is reported that Jesus had "compassion". Three times it says that He "had compassion on the multitude".[16] He had compassion on two blind men near Jericho.[17] He had compassion on a leper.[18] He had compassion on the widow of Nain.[19]

Certainly these passages reflect the tenderhearted Jesus. He could weep with sorrowing friends, take time for children and show pity to the down trodden. He was tempted in His earthly life in all points like man is tempted.[20] He understands sickness, sorrow and pain. He understands temptations from pride, lust and covetousness. Because of this He understands the plight of man and can have compassion for him. This concept is affirmed in Hebrews.

> *For since He Himself was tempted in that which He has*
> *suffered, He is able to come to the aid of those who are*
> *tempted.*[21]

It is because of the assurance that Jesus understands and cares that the Christian has confidence in approaching God through Jesus in prayer.[22]

Some have sought to make compassion one of the primary purposes of Jesus' miracles. Morton Kelsey writes thus:

> *The most important reason that Jesus healed was that He*

> *cared about people and suffered when they did. The root*
> *meaning of compassion is just this: to know suffering*
> *together.23*

Though the compassion of Jesus cannot be denied, it can hardly be one of the primary purposes of miracles. Nowhere in the New Testament does a New Testament writer indicate that compassion is the purpose of miracles. If the purpose were compassion, why did Jesus not heal more of the sick and raise more of the dead? There were a lot of sick folk around the pool of Bethesda, but He healed only one. Did not Jesus have compassion for the others? There were a lot of dead people in the cemetery when Jesus raised Lazarus, but He raised only one. Did Jesus not have compassion on the families of those others who had died?

The miracles of Jesus do indeed reflect his compassionate nature, yet this would not be one of the primary purposes of His miracles. J. W. McGarvey suggests this understanding.

> *A miracle wrought by a man is an exercise of divine power*
> *entrusted to the man for some divine purpose. When it is*
> *wrought as a mere act of mercy, the purpose may be no*
> *other than to manifest the mercy of God. But it is doubtful*
> *whether a miracle was ever wrought for this purpose alone.24*

Another secondary use of miracles is that of a teaching tool. Particularly is this seen in the Gospel of John.

After a miracle was performed by Jesus and its impact was still fresh in their minds, He would use it to teach a lesson.

Jesus used what happens in nature to illustrate spiritual truths through parables. Jesus used what happened in miracles to illustrate spiritual truths through symbolic language.

Jesus calls Himself "the bread of life" after the feeding of the five thousand. He calls Himself "the resurrection and the life" in the context of raising Lazarus from the dead. He calls Himself "the light of the world" in the context of healing the man born blind. The miracle of the barren fig tree drying up was used by Jesus to show the importance of faith.

This secondary purpose of New Testament miracles has been regarded by some as being a primary purpose.

> *Jesus' miracles were not only a primarily external*
> *confirmation of his message; rather the miracle was the*
> *vehicle of the message.*[25]

Such an understanding is not only without any support from the New Testament text, it is also contrary to the expressed purpose which is plainly stated in Scripture.

A third use of miracles was to bring publicity.[26] Although Jesus often avoided the public and sometimes instructed those He healed to "tell no man", yet news of His miracles spread abroad. This is explained in one of the miracle narratives of Mark.

> *And He gave orders not to tell anyone; but the more He ordered*
> *them, the more widely they continued to proclaim it. And they*
> *were utterly astonished, saying, He has done all things well;*
> *He makes even the deaf to hear, and the dumb to speak.*[27]

The publicity of Jesus' miracles was so widely spread that multitudes gathered around Him to witness His wonderful works. Though He often said to those who were healed, "see that no man know it"[28], yet the very nature of what was happening called people to Him.

On the day of Pentecost, the multitude came together because of the miracles that took place with the baptism of the Holy Spirit.[29] The miracle that Peter worked at the gate called Beautiful caused the people to "run together to them".[30] The miracle Paul worked at Lystra caused the people to come together.[31]

In spite of attempts by Jesus to lessen the publicity of certain miracles, it is evident that miracles in the New Testament brought attention to those who worked them. This was not their purpose, but it was one of the results of the mighty works.

It should be noted that Jesus and the apostles did not work miracles for selfish benefit. Jesus refused to turn stones into bread when He was hungry. He refused to come down from the cross or call a legion of angels to protect Him from being arrested. No miraculous power was used for His comfort or ease.

He who fed the thousands, Himself hungered. He who promised rest, Himself was weary enough to sleep in a storm tossed boat. He who turned water into wine, said, "I thirst". He who raised the dead, Himself died. He who had compassion on the multitude, left His mother with a broken heart. He who cast out demons, was Himself tempted by the Devil. There was not found a selfish purpose in any of the miracles of Jesus.

ENDNOTES

[1]See pages, pp. 27-29; 32-33; 39-40; 43-44

[2]Henry H Halley, *Bible Handbook* (Grand Rapids: Zondervan Publishing Co., 1965) p. 471

[3]John 20:30-31

[4]John 3:2

[5]Mark 16:17-20

[6]I Corinthians 12:28-31

[7]Acts 14:3 and Hebrews 2:3-4

[8]John 20:31

[9]Acts 2:1-6, see also Jimmy Jividen, *Glossolalia* (Fort Worth: Star Bible Publications, 1971) pp. 99-106

[10]Acts 2:32-33

[11]Mark 2:10-12

[12]John 4:25

[13]Matthew 11:2-5

[14]Luke 4:17-21

[15]John 7:31

[16]Matthew 9:36; 14:14; 15:32; Mark 6:34; 8:2

[17]Matthew 20:34

[18]Mark 1:41

[19]Luke 7:13

[20]Hebrews 4:15

[21]Hebrews 2:18

[22]Hebrews 4:16

[23]Morton T. Kelsey, *Healing and Christianity* (New York: Harper and Row, 1976) pp. 88-89

[24]John William McGarvey, *Biblical Criticism* (Nashville: Gospel Advocate Company, 1956) p. 354

[25]Raymond E. Brown, *The Jerome Biblical Commentary* (Englewood Cliffs, N. J.: Prentice Hall, 1968) p. 787

[26]Matthew 8:4; Mark 7:36; Luke 5:14

[27]Mark 7:36-37

[28]Matthew 9:30; Mark 5:43

[29]Acts 2:6

[30]Acts 3:11

[31]Acts 14:11

CHAPTER 8

NEW TESTAMENT MIRACLES AND PAGAN WONDERS

To understand the uniqueness of the New Testament miracles, one must place them in the context of the first century world into which they came. The claim of the miraculous was no new thing for the culture in which Jesus and the apostles lived. They were communicating with people who had all kinds of notions of spirits, demons and gods. Claims of the miraculous were common.

First Century Wonder Workers

The Jews of Jesus' day had a rich background in the miraculous. The Old Testament Scriptures contain the miracles of Moses, Elijah and Elisha and random signs scattered throughout their history. Most of the miracles occurred during the time of special revelation and served to confirm the prophet and his prophecy as being from God. The miraculous was involved in the ministries of Moses, Daniel, and others. Holy men of God spoke as they were moved by the Holy Spirit. God also confirmed their message with signs.

Besides the Old Testament miracles, there were many claims of the miraculous in Jewish history. The Apocrypha speak of all kinds of miracles being done by Jewish heroes.

An example of this is found in Tobit. When Tobias and his company came to the Tigris river "a fish leaped up from the river and would have swallowed the young man . . .". The fish was caught and eaten. The heart, liver and gall of the fish were saved. It was to be carried on their journey. The angel, Azarias, was asked what it was to be used for. His reply inferred that it was to cure blindness and drive away demons.

> *He replied, 'As for the heart and the liver, if a demon or evil*
> *spirit gives trouble to any one, you make a smoke from*
> *these before the man or woman, and that person will never*
> *be troubled again. And as for the gall, anoint with it a man*
> *who has white films in his eyes, and he will be cured'.[1]*

The Jews of Jesus' day had a background both in true and false wonders. With such a background no wonder Paul said that ""for indeed Jews ask for signs . . ."[2]

The Roman culture of the first century was diverse.

On one extreme there were men like Cicero who denounced divination as a superstition. He claimed that such claims took advantage of human weakness and cast a spell over the mind of man.

To the other extreme the miracle stories surrounding the Roman emperors were many. Tacitus writes of Vespasian being connected with healing a blind man in Alexandria. He put spittle in his eyes, and they were healed. He also healed a man with a crippled hand by walking on it. These miracles were associated with his visit to the Sarapeum. According to Tacitus, this shows that Sarapis gave divine approval to Vespasian.

The Greek world of the first century was dualistic. There was the world of matter and the world of the spirit. Man was both mind (*nous*) and body (*physis*) The mind was trapped in the body which was material, non-essential and passing away. This dualism was to present major problems in the church under the guise of what would later be called Gnosticism. This dualistic view of nature and man along with the nature of the Greek gods made miracles the expected thing.

Devotees of the mystery religions expected the supernatural to seize them in the religious rituals. Miracle stories were told about their heroes. Healing shrines and oracle shrines were popular. Priests were skilled in producing experiences by psychological manipulation. Bloody sacrifices, sacred snakes, mysterious language, mood changing music and sacred rituals all combined to make their religion very experiential.

The claim of the miracle of inspiration was common. The gods spoke through the oracles. Oracle shrines were common. Slaves and emperors visited these shrines to learn the will of the gods and discover the future. E. R. Dodds writes of the oracles at Delphi.

> *At Delphi, and apparently at most of his oracles, Apollo relied, not on visions . . . but on 'enthusiasm' in its original and literal sense. The Pythis became <u>enteos plena deo:</u> the god entered into her and used her vocal organs as if they were his own. . .3*

The miracle of healing was also very common. Shrines of Esklepios were scattered throughout the Greek world. Healing was a combination of psyche suggestions, religious ritual, drugs and physical therapy. Modern medicine traces some of its roots back to some medical skills which came from this cult of Esklepios. A number of the museums today have on display many of the artifacts which one time filled these shrines. They reflect healings of all kinds of illnesses and injuries.

It was into such a wonder working world that Jesus came. There were claimsof miracles from Greeks, Romans and Jews. The whole culture had in its psyche the direct intervention of the gods into the affairs of men. Jesus was to bring in a different kind of miracle. It would be real and not a pious priestly fraud. It would be factual, not exaggerated fantasy. It would be indisputable even from His enemies.

Jesus' miracles and those of the apostolic company were unique.

New Testament Evidence

From the New Testament itself, one is able to discover much information about the pagan miracles of the first century. The miracles of Jesus and the apostolic company must be compared to and contrasted with the claims of the pagan wonders.

One of the most notable pagan wonder workers in the New Testament is Simon the Magician. Luke describes him thus:

> *Now there was a certain man named Simon, who formerly*

> *was practicing magic in the city, and astonishing the people*
> *of Samaria, claiming to be someone great; and they all, from*
> *the smallest to the greatest, were giving attention to him,*
> *saying, 'This man is what is called Great Power of God'.*
> *And they were giving him attention because he had for a long*
> *time astonished them with the magic arts.*[4]

The miracles of Philip were so much greater than his magic that Simon was converted.[5] He had a hard time giving up his old ways. He wanted the power that the apostles had of laying hands on individuals and giving them the Holy Spirit. Peter rebuked him and demanded that he repent. Luke does not finish the story as to whether he repented or not. He does, however, show that money and miracles go together in the mind of those with bad hearts. Ecclesiastical tradition has Simon becoming a false teacher in the early church. Eusebius said that he was the author of all heresy.

Elymas Bar-Jesus was another magician confronted by Paul and Barnabas. Luke describes him as a false prophet who was in company with Sergius Paulus, the proconsul of Salamis. He opposed Barnabas and Saul and tried to turn the proconsul away from their teaching. He was resisted by Paul and struck blind. Paul's rebuke tells something of him.

> *You who are full of all deceit and fraud, you son of the devil*
> *you enemy of all righteousness, will you not cease to make*
> *crooked the straight ways of the Lord?*[6]

Paul had no hesitancy in exposing one who by deceit and fraud turned people away from the truth.

An unnamed damsel at Philippi had a spirit of divination which she used to tell fortunes.[7] When Paul arrived at Philippi, she began to follow him saying, "These men are bond-servants of the Most High God, who are proclaiming to you the way of salvation". Paul cast the evil spirit out of her. Her masters were angry because they saw that their hope of profit was gone. They put Paul and Silas in prison.

If there was ever a time to compromise with a false religion, it would appear to be here at Philippi. After all, she was speaking the truth when she identified Paul and Silas as servants of the Most High God.

Religious toleration would have been satisfied if Paul and Silas had left things like they were. Certainly they would not have been jailed if they had not confronted the false religion. This incident shows that followers of Jesus Christ do not give sanction to or compromise with those who teach or practice a false doctrine. Resisting evil or false spirits is just as much a part of evangelism as is the affirmation of the true Gospel.

The seven sons of Sceva were Jewish exorcists who were operating in Ephesus during Paul's stay there.

> *But there were some of the Jewish exorcists, who went from place to place, attempting to name over those who had evil spirits the name of the Lord Jesus, saying, 'I adjure you by Jesus whom Paul preaches'. And the seven sons of one Sceva, a Jewish chief priest, were doing this. And the evil spirit answered and said to them, 'I recognize Jesus, and I know about Paul, but who are you?'. And the man in whom was the evil spirit leaped on them and subdued both of them and overpowered them, so that they fled out of that house naked and wounded.[8]*

Exorcism was very common in the first century. The Paris Magical Papyrus is an example of the formula which was used to supposedly cast out demons. The Papyrus is dated about 300 A. D. but reflects times much earlier also.

> *I adjure thee by the god of the Hebrews Jesu, Jaba, Jae, Abraoth, Aia, Thoth, Ele, Aeo, Eu, Jiibaech, Abarmas, Jabarau, Abelbel, Lona, Abra, Maroia, arm, thou that appearest in fire, thou that art in the midst of earth and snow and vapor, Tannetis: let thy angel descend, the implacable one, and let him draw into captivity the demon as he flieth in his holy paradise.[9]*

It is easy to see the Jewish and the Christian influence on the exorcist's formula. Any name that might help their magic was welcomed. It must not have been uncommon for Jews to take up this practice. Such was the case in the Ephesus incident. Jesus refers to the practice of exorcism associated with such an orthodox body as the Pharisees. He responded to their accusation that Jesus was casting out demons by Beelzebul, by asking "by whom do your sons cast them out?".[10]

Again this passage shows the incompatibility of those who follow Jesus and those who work wonders by pagan standard.

A classic example of the effect of the Gospel on those who practice the magic arts is found in another incident in the city of Ephesus.

> *And many of those who practiced magic brought their books together, and began burning them in the sight of all; and they counted up the price of them and found it fifty thousand pieces of silver.*[11]

Christians at Ephesus, who formerly practiced magic, demonstrated their repentance by destroying their books of magic. Luke said the cost was fifty thousand pieces of silver, which would be about $1,160,000 in current value. They burned their bridges behind them when they became Christians and removed from themselves the temptation to return to their old pagan ways. Again this incident affirms that Christianity is incompatible with the practice of magic, deceitful signs and false wonders.

Paul makes reference to pagan worship practices in correcting the abuse of spiritual gifts in the Corinthian correspondence.

> *You know that when you were pagans, you were led astray to the dumb idols, however you were led.*[12]

It would appear from the context that the abuse of the miraculous gift of speaking in other languages was not unlike pagan ecstasy. In pagan worship people were "led astray" because they surrendered their will to an experience. In this experience they cared little for understanding and often did the irrational. Particularly was this true in the Greek mystery religions. What the Corinthian Christians were doing looked much like these pagan practices. They were speaking in foreign languages which neither they nor the people who were listening could understand. They were doing it all at the same time. No one was translating the language into rational meaning so that the assembly could be edified. The confusion resembled the irrational ecstasy of the pagan mysteries.

It is no wonder that Paul begins his correction of the abuse of spiritual gifts by suggesting that what they were doing was more pagan than Christian. Such irrational experiential behavior is incompatible with the real power of the Holy Spirit and the rational meaning that comes from the right use of the spiritual gifts.

One incident in the Gospels does not fit into the pattern of miracles performed by the apostles or Jesus Himself. Neither does it fit into the discussion of pagan wonders. The incident is recorded by both Mark and Luke.

> *John said to Him, Teacher, we saw someone casting out*
> *demons in Your name, and we tried to hinder him because*
> *he was not following us. But Jesus said, Do not hinder him,*
> *for there is no one who shall perform a miracle in My*
> *name, and be able soon afterward to speak evil of Me.*
> *For he who is not against us is for us.[13]*

There are many problems in understanding this text. Why was such an individual casting out demons in the name of Jesus if he were not following him? Jesus had already condemned those who claimed to cast out demons and refused to do his will.[14] What was the source of his power? It would appear that Jesus acknowledged that he had worked a miracle in casting out demons. He was not an apostle. It seems unlikely that he was among the seventy that Jesus sent out.[15] How does this passage conform to the attempt that the seven sons of Sceva made to cast out demons in the name of Jesus?[16] The seven sons of Sceva were viewed with disapproval in Luke's account in Acts. The one whom John asked about was not to be hindered.

One must not try to explain this passage away because it is difficult. There are some observations which should be made.

First, the purpose of this story is to be seen in the context. The apostles were having problems with pride of rank and prejudice against the weak. Jesus showed them that the servant was the greatest, children were not to be rejected and even the Samaritans were not to be despised. The miraculous element seems to be only incidental.

Second, Jesus does not give either sanction or rejection to the one who John said were casting out demons in Jesus' name. Jesus just observes that those who used His name to cast out demons could not be against Him.

Third, there is not enough information given in the text to know who this man was or by what means he was able to cast out demons. It would be presumptuous to say more than that which is written. Everett

Ferguson shows such caution in commenting on this passage.

> *We do not know whether this "strange exorcist" as he has*
> *been called, was a disciple of Jesus apart from the twelve*
> *who had been commissioned by Jesus, a prospective disciple*
> *in a stage of transition whom Jesus encouraged, or a*
> *wandering free-lance practitioner who had observed the*
> *success of Jesus and his disciples on other occasions and had*
> *picked up the name of Jesus (in which case his success may*
> *have been allowed by God in order to enhance the reputation*
> *and respect for the name of Jesus).[17]*

Asklepios

Howard Clark Kee in his book, *Miracle in the Early Christian World*, has
collected and interpreted a remarkable amount of material showing the
thought-world of that time period.[18] Miracles were involved in most religions from the Emperor's cult to Sarapis' shrines. Kee chooses two of the
most prominent to serve as examples, Asklepios and Isis.

One can not discuss miracles in the first century without examining the most famous of the Greek healing gods, Asklepios. We are fortu-
nate to have information concerning the cult from both literary sources
and archaeological discoveries. There are well preserved shrines of
Asklepios in both ancient Cos and Epidaurus. In the museum at ancient
Corinth, a large room is filled with artifacts discovered from the
Corinthian Asklepion. These artifacts include legs, arms, ears, eyes and
other parts of the body which the devotee thought had been healed.
These were *ex votos* gifts. They had been given in fulfillment of a vow
or as a thank offering for healing.

From the literature, the shrines, and the artifacts, the following is
a composite of what seemed to be the process by which the devotees
sought healing:

There was a sacrifice of small animals in the section containing
the altar. This structure is evident at Epidaurus. There were ritual bath-
ings from a sacred spring which seemed to be associated with each of the
shrines. Near the Asklepion there was located an amphitheater where
drama would be added to the ritual involved in the healing process. A

basic factor in seeking healing at the Asklepion was spending the night in the Abaton. After making an offering and washing in the sacred spring, the devotee would go to the Abaton to spend the night. Here he was expected to have a vision of Asklepios who would advise him of the method of treatment.

Different shrines seemed to emphasize different aspects of the Asklepios tradition. Excavations at Cos indicate a strong emphasis on the medical arts while excavations at Epidaurus indicate an emphasis on the direct divine intervention in healing. Kee writes the following:

> *Not only is there no hint (at Epidauros jj) in the accounts*
> *of healing that a medical procedure was actually followed,*
> *but in the excavations there was no trace of surgical*
> *equipment. At Cos, on the other hand, where Asklepios was*
> *linked with the developing medical school tradition, were*
> *found an operating theater, with all its instruments and*
> *apparatus, levels of all kinds and beams to help reset*
> *dislocated bones, knives, trephines and instruments for*
> *cutting the uvula, as well as sick rooms and facilities for*
> *apothecaries. By contrast, at Epidauros, the healings were*
> *wholly matters of divine operation.[19]*

It was from such shrines as Cos that medical knowledge was preserved and developed. Galen, one of the most important figures in the history of medicine, received his education at Pergamum and Smyrna. Both were centers of the Asklepios cult. Though Galen's emphasis was more along the line of Hippocrates and the experimental practice of medicine, yet the influence of the Asklepios traditions cannot be overlooked.

Sacred snakes, which were believed to be the visible form of Asklepios, were associated with the healing ceremonies. These snakes, according to the literary evidence, lived in the confines of the Asklepion and were used by the priests in prescribing cures. Kee describes what it must have been like in the Abaton.

> *The pilgrims were required to spend the night within the*
> *shrine, so that they might receive communications from the*
> *god, either directly by an epiphany or indirectly through dreams,*
> *or by an intermediary in the form of a dog or snake. It is*
> *easy to imagine the vigil of the suppliants, lying in the total*

> *darkness of the abaton, listening for the padding of the feet*
> *of the priests or sacred dogs, or nearly noiseless slithering*
> *of sacred snakes.*[20]

Judging from the number of Asklepions discovered from the ancient
Graeco-Roman world, their rich adornment, the written evidence of trav-
elers and historians and the numerous artifacts and inscriptions from faithful devotees, one must confess that "divine" healing by Asklepios was a
very important part of the first century world.

Isis

The worship of Isis, an Egyptian deity, goes back to the fourth millen-
nium B. C. Her function as a healing goddess does not become prominent until Hellenistic and Roman times. During this period she was
closely connected with Sarapis, a god thought to be of Semitic origin
which appealed to Greek and Hellenized Egyptians. The great Sarapeum
in Alexandria was erected in the third century B. C. Reference of
healings and miracles becomes more prominent from this time.

Much can be learned about the worship of Isis through an
aretalogy from the writings of Diodorus Siculus.

> *The Egyptians say that she was the discoverer of many health*
> *giving drugs and was greatly versed in the science of*
> *healing; consequently, now that she has attained immorality,*
> *she finds her greatest delight in the healing of mankind and*
> *gives aid in their sleep to those who call upon her. . .*
>
> *. . . For standing above the sick in their sleep she gives aid*
> *for their diseases and works remarkable cures upon such as*
> *submit themselves to her; and many who have been despaired*
> *of by their physicians because of the difficult nature of their*
> *malady are restored to health by her.*[21]

By the time that Lucius Apuleius wrote *Metamorphoses* much of the
emphasis in the worship of Isis was that of obtaining a new "life orienta-
tion", but healing is still involved.[22] Apuleius was healed. He was

changed from an ass to a human, even though this appears to be more of a symbol of an inward change which took place in him.

During the first century the healing emphasis of worship of Isis was still prominent. It formed a part of the "life-world" into which the miracles of Jesus came.

Pagan and New Testament Miracles Contrasted

It becomes quite evident in the examination of healing miracles of Isis and Asklepios that they are different from those in the New Testament. There is a distinct similarity between the practices surrounding the cult of Asklepios and the healing claims of Roman Catholicism in the middle ages or the contemporary claims which come from Fatima.

One needs to note these differences between the pagan miracles and those contained in the New Testament.

First, the environment in which the miracle takes place is quite different. The environment of the New Testament miracles did not tune the psyche to receive an experience through rituals, drugs or drama. The surroundings were not mystical or designed to produce a degree of ecstasy.

There were no holy springs, sleeping on holy ground with dogs, snakes and priests passing by in the darkness. New Testament miracles happened without dramatic build up or artificially controlled environment.

Second, the success rate was different. The shrines of Asklepios provided a means in which some susceptible individuals would have a vision of a cure. But think of the ones who would go away with no relief from their affliction. Some shrines like Cos developed medical means of helping the gods heal. This is confirmed by the artifacts found in the excavation of the the ancient sites. New Testament miracle workers were always successful. The one exception being the failure of the apostles to heal an epileptic due to their lack of faith.[23] New Testament workers of miracles did not require help through the practice of the science of medicine. Their miracles were the direct act of God.

Third, the purpose was different. The purpose of healing at the shrines of Asklepios was an end within itself. People came to be healed. The ritual focused on healing. Votive offerings were given in gratitude for healing. The shrine and the priest were richly rewarded for their service. The purpose of the New Testament miracles was to be a sign to point to the men or the message as being from God. John Locke observed that he did not remember "any miracle recorded in the Greek or Roman writers, as done to confirm anyone's mission or doctrine".[24] New Testament miracles were not an end within themselves. Those who performed the miracles were not enriched in the process.

Fourth, the believability of the healings is different. It is easy to discern some of the psychological factors involved with the healings claimed in the name of Asklepios. The power of suggestion, the mood altering environment of the shrine and the psychosomatic nature of so many illnesses cause one to doubt the cures at the Asklepion. The use of drugs, herbs, diets and baths were all used in a very non-miraculous way to effect cures. This cannot be said of the New Testament miracles. The cures were immediate, full, direct and without the use of supplementary means.

It should be observed that the elements which make the healings of Asklepios different from the New Testament miracles are the same ones which make the claims of contemporary miracles different from the New Testament healings.

ENDNOTES

[1]Tobit 6:7-8

[2]I Corinthians 1:22

[3]E.R. Dodds, The Greeks and the Irrational
(Boston: Beacon Press, 1957) pp.   70-71

[4]Acts 8:9-10

[5]Acts 8:13

[6]Acts 13:10

[7]Acts 16:16-23

[8]Acts 19:13-16

[9]C. K. Barrett, *The New Testament Background: Selected Documents* (London: S. P. C. K.,1956) p. 32

[10]Matthew 12:27

[11]Acts 19:19

[12]I Corinthians 12:2

[13]Mark 9:38-40 see also Luke 9:49-50

[14]Matthew 7:21-23

[15]Luke 10:1-20

[16]Acts 19:13-16

[17]Everett Ferguson, *Demonology of the Early Christian World* (New York: The Edwin Mellen Press, 1984) p. 15

[18]Howard Clark Kee, *Miracle in the Early Christian World* (New Haven: Yale University Press, 1983)

[19]Kee, *op. cit.*, p. 86

[20]Kee, *op. cit.*, p. 85

[21]Diodorus Siculus (Loeb Classical Library l. 25. 3, 5)

[22]Kee, *op. cit.*, pp. 132-145

[23]Matthew 17:19

[24]John Locke, *The Reasonableness of Christianity* (Chicago: Henry Regnery Company, 1965) p. 208

CHAPTER 9

GOD'S WORK IN THE WORLD TODAY

There is a temptation for one to react negatively to all of frauds in religion and the brassy claims of those who claim divine miracles. In such a reaction one might put God "way out there" like the Deists. He might view God as unconcerned with the plight of man or unable to influence the natural order of the universe to help him. Such a reaction is as dangerous as the error it seeks to overcome.

One can not relegate Jesus to the dusty pages of history or view His work as impersonal and irrelevant to the contemporary world. He lives today. He is not unconcerned with man. After all, He left heaven for man's sake. Surely Jesus will not forget man's plight after identifying with man on earth.

One cannot identify the Holy Spirit with the text of the Scriptures and de-conceptualize Him as being a real person. One cannot see His work as being a one time activity of the first century. He still lives today. He acts and will continue to act in the world until Jesus comes.

Why Men Reject God's Work in the World

There is a temptation to ignore or minimize God's activity in the world for several reasons.

First, there are so many claims made in the name of religion which promise quick fixes for long standing problems and short cuts to spirituality, that many have been turned off from anything spiritual.

The hoopla experientialism of charismatic religion is short lived and shallow. The sociological saturation of the Church Growth Movement has humanized and secularized much of what happens in the name of religion. Egocentric, psychologically oriented, self help humanism is often found clothed in religious terms and so called spiritual outreaches. Observing all of this in today's world, many have put God on the shelf as an old, worn-out superstition.

Even this book, with its rejection of contemporary miraculous claims, can be wrongly used as a barrier to discovering the real workings of God in the world. It is not so intended. It's purpose is to expose the false, the frauds and the deluding fantasies so that one might see the true activity of God in all of its glory.

God does work in the world today. Jesus promised that He would be with His disciples always.[1] God still works all things according to the counsel of His will.[2] The Holy Spirit is still able to do exceedingly abundant above all that we ask or think.[3]

Second, man feels himself to have outgrown the need of God. He does not contemplate how God is silently working in the universe to sustain His laws.[4] He does not thank God for his abilities, his opportunities or his circumstances which he has received by the grace of God. He does not consider that even the bread he eats is still a blessing of God, even if he has labored to earn it.

Ingratitude led to idolatry among the Gentiles of Paul's day, and it will do the same today. Their idols were made of stone, but the most popular god of contemporary man is ego. In writing about how the Gentiles had gone into idolatry and immorality, Paul shows that the first step was ingratitude. They thought that they no longer needed God.

> *For even though they knew God, they did not honor Him as God, or give thanks; but they became futile in their speculations, and their foolish heart was darkened. Professing to be wise, they became fools . . .*[5]

The self-sufficiency of man, then and now, is the first step away from God. There is no greater idol than the idol of man's own ego.

Jesus told a parable of the rich fool who spoke and acted as though he did not need God. After a bountiful harvest he said, "Soul, you have many goods laid up for many years to come; take your ease, eat, drink and be merry".[6] Jesus called such a man a "fool". He was a fool because he thought that he did not need God.

Third, man does not understand how God works in the world. He thinks that God only works in ways that are positive to man. He thinks that the ugly, the bad and the evil are evidence that God cannot or will not act in the affairs of men. They only want to see the sunny side of God. If God acts in judgment, it is too severe to be God's work. If God allows the consequences of man breaking His laws to be bad, it is too severe to be God's work. If God, in allowing man his free will, permits sin and evil, then such is too negative to be God's work.

The god of positive thinking is too small. The god of goodness only is too narrow. The god of grace only is too limited. The god of blessing only is inadequate. The God of Grace is also the God of Law. The God of Goodness is also the God of Judgment. The God of Blessing is also the God of Adversity. Paul expressed the breadth of God's being thus:

> *Behold then the kindness and severity of God; to those who fell, severity, but to you, God's kindness, if you continue in His kindness; otherwise you also will be cut off.[7]*

One should not deny the activity of God in the world just because his view of God is small. It is a little presumptuous for the pot to tell the potter how he should make pots. If one limits the activity of God to only that which he thinks is worthy of God, then he has made another idol.

> *Oh the depth of the riches both of the wisdom and knowledge of God! How unsearchable are His judgments and unfathomable His ways! **For who has known the mind of the Lord, or who became His counselor?**[8]*

The Scriptures affirm and experience confirms that there are ways in which God still works in the world.

Nature

One is able to see the workings of God in nature. God did not create the world by His power and then cut off that power. He continues to sustain the world to this present day. If for one moment God's sustaining power would cease, then the universe would disintegrate into the nothingness from which it was created. In discussing the person and work of Jesus, the author of Hebrews shows that just as Jesus was the source of creation, He is also the source of upholding this creation to the present time.

> . . .*His Son, whom He appointed heir of all things, through whom also He made the world. And He is the radiance of His glory and the exact representation of His nature, and upholds all things by the word of His power.*[9]

In creation God made *kosmos,* or order. This *kosmos* was made possible by certain laws which govern the universe. The planets stay in their orbits. The sea stays within its bounds. The seasons follow a certain order. A seed brings forth after its kind. These laws of nature do not - exist in and of themselves. The God who spoke them into existence sustains their orderliness by His constant power. Just as a machine does not function of and by itself, the created universe is not a self-sustaining system. Both a machine and the universe can not function without the care of him who created it.

Paul affirms that one cannot separate the activity of God in creation from His work in sustaining this creation.

> *And He is the image of the invisible God, the firstborn of all creation. For in Him all things were created, both in the heavens and on earth, visible and invisible, whether thrones or dominions or rulers or authorities --- all things have been created through Him and for Him. And He is before all things, and in Him all things hold together.*[10]

To suggest that God has ceased to work in the world because there is no longer Divine inspiration or confirming miracles is to know only one small aspect of God's being and power. Such a god is too small. Such a god is not the God revealed in the Bible, but merely another idol of man.

If God does not still work in nature, why would one pray for daily bread? Why would one want to thank Him for His gracious care? If God does not still work in the world, then what good is there in praying for the sick or asking God's blessings upon those who rule in human governments?

God is no less active when He works according to the natural order of the universe. It is an act of God when any sickness is cured, even though it is done according to the laws that are understood by man. It is no less an act of God that the doctor is able to use physical therapy, drugs, diet or surgery to bring about the cure. The doctor just brings the laws of God together for man's benefit. He is not the healer but only a means through whom God heals.

Prayer

One is able to see the working of God in answered prayer. God hears and answers every prayer.

> *And this is the confidence which we have before Him,*
> *that, if we ask anything according to His will, He hears us.[11]*

He might not always answer the prayer according to the preference of the one praying, but He does answer. Fathers often do not give their children what they ask for. What they want might not be what they need. What they want might be immature wishing or unhealthy desires. Just as a father is selective in fulfilling the request of his children, God is selective in granting the request of His children's prayers.[12]

Prayer is not only seeking to get God to yield to our petitions, it is just as much a yielding of our will to His purpose. Like Jesus taught and practiced, the first desire of prayer is "Thy will be done".[13]

It has become easy in the contemporary culture for man to feel self- sufficient and in control. He has discovered so many of the laws which govern the universe that he can do wondrous things. He does not need God. By working within the framework of these laws, he can be prosperous, healthy and satisfied. The problem is that he is not satisfied even with wealth and prosperity. He involves himself with the laws of the universe, but has forgotten the Lawgiver. He has left out the Divine dimension of life and is unsatisfied.

When man leaves God out, his plans will fail and his desires will not be fulfilled. There will exist within him a "God-shaped void" which longs for fulfillment.

James teaches that one should take God into his confidence in planning for the future. It is folly not to. One's life is fragile and fleeting and he can not even know if he will be alive tomorrow. One cannot know the future or if what he plans will be good or bad. One is ignorant of the will of God and is presumptuous to think that he knows what is best for himself in the future.

> *Come now, you who say, 'Today or tomorrow, we shall go to such and such a city, and spend a year there and engage in business and make a profit'. Yet you do not know what your life will be like tomorrow, You are just a vapor that appears for a little while and than vanishes away. Instead, you ought to say, 'If the Lord wills, we shall live and also do this or that.*[14]

Prayer enables one to plan with God. God works in the world to help such planning find fulfillment.

James teaches that it is folly to desire without asking God for help in obtaining these desires. "You do not have because you do not ask"[15] is a sobering judgment upon a man who is frustrated in striving for goals which he has not been able to reach.

Prayer enables one to have the help of God in accomplishing the things he wants to do and having the things he desires to have. God works in the world for His children to bring about that which is good for them. But they need to ask.

One does not have to know how it is that God answers every prayer. He does not need to know why God's answers do not always fit the pattern that he thinks is best. It is enough to know that the God who loves him and cares about his needs is in control. He will always do what is best for His children.

> *Ask and it shall be given to you; seek, and you shall find; knock, and it shall be opened to you. For every one who asks receives; and he who seeks finds; and to him who knocks it shall be opened. Or what man is there among you, when his son shall ask him for a loaf, will give him a stone? Or if he shall ask for a fish, he will not give him a snake, will he? If you then, being evil, know how to give good gifts to your children, how much more shall your Father who is in heaven give what is good to those who ask Him.*[16]

To deny that God is working in the world today is to nullify the power and purpose of prayer. If God does not actively respond to one's petition, then prayer is no more than talking into the wind.

Providence

One is able to see the working of God in the world today through what is sometimes called "providence". The word "providence" is from the Latin, *providentia*, which means "foresight". The Greek word, *pronoia*, means "to provide".

It is used in the New Testament two times but has little in common with the contemporary use of the term.[17]

In the Septuagint, *pronoia*, was used to mean almost the same thing as God. This was also similar to the way Hellenistic writers of the time used the word.

The meaning is the activity of God to direct and overrule events. This activity is not arbitrary, but in conformance with His creation. Both human history and nature are the sphere of this Divinely determined activity. The object of the providence is God's predetermined plan which he foresees and wills. J. D. Thomas has defined "providence" as " a non-revelational behind-the-scene action of God in history".[18]

Though the contemporary use of the word is not found in the New Testament, the meaning it conveys is found often. God did not create the world and then let it run on its own without further Divine intervention. He intervened in special ways in the history of Israel. He intervened in the world in sending Jesus, in establishing the Church and will intervene again when Jesus comes. These interventions were special and often accompanied with the miraculous.

There is another way, however, in which God continues to intervene in the affairs of men. This intervention is not miraculous, but providential. God's will is accomplished, but it is through the natural process of the laws which govern the universe.

God still rules in the kingdoms of men and gives them to whomever He desires.[19] The powers that be are ordained of God.[20] Jesus' reply to Pilate's boast that he had power to release or crucify Him was "You would have no authority over Me, unless it had been given you from above".[21] These passages show that God continues to control the governments of the world, even though it might be done through military might or the democratic process. It is no less an activity of God if He chooses to accomplish His will through natural means. Nations rise and fall by the present workings of God in the world. God still controls the destiny of nations.

Throughout history one is able to see that God has worked in natural ways to bring about His will for men.

This is shown in the story of Esther. She was able to save the Jews because she was in the right place at the right time with the right influence. Mordecai asked an important question of her when he was seeking her intervention on behalf of the Jews before Ahasuerus.

And who knows whether you have not attained royalty
for such a time as this.[22]

This is shown in the story of Joseph being raised to power in Egypt. Joseph recognized that his position was not due to his power and might but to the providence of God. God was working in the triumphs and tragedies of his life to accomplish the preservation of Abraham's seed. His statement to his brothers shows this.

And now do not be grieved or angry with yourselves, because
you sold me here; for God sent me before you to preserve
life. . . .Now, therefore, it was not you who sent me here,
but God; and He has made me a father to Pharaoh and lord
of all his household and ruler over all the land of Egypt.[23]

Paul shows the providential workings of God even in the evil rule of the Pharaoh of Egypt. God worked to bring about the right person in the right place at the right time to bring about the Exodus. This is the teaching of Paul's statement in Romans.

For the Scriptures says to Pharaoh, for this very purpose I
raised you up, to demonstrate my power in you, that
my name might be proclaimed throughout the whole
earth.[24]

God still intervenes in the affairs of individual men, even though one is not quite sure how He does or when He does. Paul spoke of such probable Divine intervention in the lives of Philemon and Onesimus. Onesimus Philemon's runaway slave, was converted by Paul in Rome. After his conversion he was sent back to Philemon with an epistle. In the epistle Paul writes about what is sometimes called the "providential perhaps".

> *For perhaps, he was for this reason parted from you for a*
> *while, that you should have him back forever, no longer as a*
> *slave, but more than a slave, a beloved brother . . .*[25]

One should note that Paul does not claim absolute knowledge of God working in bringing about the conversion of Onesimus and his return to Philemon, he merely says, "perhaps". One should be cautious in calling the shots for God in how and when he is working in the world today. It can be said that, "perhaps God used the tragedy of World War II in order to bring about a greater zeal to evangelize the world". It would be presumptuous for one to state such without qualifying it with "perhaps". It is not an absolute indisputable fact that this was such a providential intervention of God.

The Christian has confidence in the workings of God in the world. He can say, "The Lord is my helper"[26] and know that it is a present reality. The help of the Lord is more than some vague future hope. God still lives and acts.

The Christian can resist temptation with strength that is beyond that which comes from sheer will and natural ability. He has the promised help of God.

> *No temptation has overtaken you but such as is common*
> *to man; and God is faithful, who will not allow you to be*
> *tempted beyond what you are able; but with the temptation*
> *will provide the way of escape also, that you may be able to*
> *endure it.*[27]

God continues to act in the world today in providing Christians a way of escape from temptation. This is more than merely the nature of things as they are in the world. It is rather God's intervention in a providential way on behalf of His children.

The Christian can endure temporary struggles, personal tragedy and extreme adversity because he knows that there is purpose in it all.

God has promised to make the ultimate end "good" no matter how bad things look or how great the opposition. Paul states such a promise.

> *And we know that God causes all things to work together*
> *for good to those who love God, to those who are called*
> *according to His purpose . . . What then shall we say to these*
> *things? If God is for us, who is against us? He who did not*
> *spare His own Son, but delivered Him up for us all, how*
> *will He not also with Him freely give us all things?*[28]

God is alive and well in the world today. He promises to be with those who love Him and will give them good things. He promises that He will make the end beautiful. This confidence is not merely positive thinking or devout wishing, it is experienced in the real everyday, workaday world.

The Christian does not need to worry about physical things which absorb so much energy as those without God's help. Jesus, in His sermon on materialism, tells His disciples not to worry about food and clothes. God knows one's needs and will provide for His children.

> *Do not be anxious then, saying, What shall we eat? or What*
> *shall we drink? or With what shall we clothe ourselves? For*
> *all these things the Gentiles eagerly seek; for your heavenly*
> *Father knows that you need all these things. But seek first*
> *His kingdom and His righteousness; and all these things shall*
> *be added to you.*[29]

One might not know how God is going to do this in times of economic depression or social strife, but the Christian believes that God will find a way. The provisions of God might not be all that a person might want or thinks he needs, but it will be sufficient. More is involved in this than mere hard work and a sharp mind. God in a real way opens doors, gives wisdom, provides strength and blesses the efforts of those who are His children.

The New Testament teaches that God still works in the world in a real way. In affirming this, one must be careful not to go beyond what is written. By faith, the Christian knows that God is concerned for every individual man. By faith, the Christian knows that God still works in the world. The Christian must also understand that it is impossible for him in some mysterious way to always know when and how God is working.

The providence of God is seen in both opportunities men receive and in the sufferings which they endure. God still controls the world and all that goes on in it.

In a very special way God is presently working in Christians. Paul affirms that God works in us to will and do His good pleasure.[30]

Christ works in the Christian's life to give him power beyond the ordinary.[31] The Holy Spirit also works in the Christian's life. It was the Holy Spirit which Paul says is the power which enables the Christian to "do exceedingly abundantly beyond all that we ask or think".[32] The Christian can affirm that God is still working in His people.

Chaos or Kosmos

How is it that one can deny contemporary miracles and at the same time affirm that God still acts in the world. The question is not "Does God act?" but "How does God act?". God does not have to work miracles to be active in the affairs of men or in upholding the laws of nature.

It is just as much the working of God that an acorn makes an oak in nature as it was when God first created the oak tree. It is just as much the working of God when a sick person is cured through the natural processes by which the body overcomes disease as it was when Jesus healed the sick.

The source and the power is the same, but the means are different. In the creation of the heavens and earth, God established certain laws by which the world would be ordered. The seed was to bring forth after its kind. The waters above were separated from the waters beneath. A multitude of consistent, observable patterns came into being which is often referred to as "nature" or "the laws of nature".

In the creation narrative it is said that at the beginning there was chaos . . . "the earth was waist and void"[33] From this chaos, God brought order. God saw that it was good.

One of the terms the Greeks used for "world" was *kosmos* which means "well ordered". They recognized that there was order in the world. It was from this presupposition that they were able to begin the development of the what was later called the "scientific method". The scientific method rests on the assumption that there is order in the universe.

This understanding is relevant in the discussion of miracles of the New Testament. A miracle happens when God breaks into the orderliness of His laws of creation with power beyond the normal in order to give a sign of confirmation to that in the spiritual realm. When men see such an activity of God, they are filled with wonder and are motivated to believe. Basic to the New Testament miracles is that they are "out of harmony" with normal happenings. They are chaotic in regard to the consistent orderly flow of the *kosmos* They are inconsistent with the laws of nature as man perceives them.

They are in harmony with God's eternal purpose. They even might be in harmony with God's greater realm of the spirit. According to the natural order of things in the world, however, they are out of harmony. Miracles might be said to be the activity of God "out of harmony" with the laws He spoke into existence at creation.

There is also the activity of God which is in harmony with the laws of creation. Both are the activity of God. Both reveal His concern for man.

God works in nature, in providence, in answering prayers and in determining the rise and fall of nations. This He does "in harmony" with His laws of creation. God has worked in history through miracles that are "out of harmony" with His laws of creation. One must not think of one being greater than the other. Both are Divine activity. Both declare God's glory.

It is not a rejection of God's power or presence in the world to deny contemporary miraculous claims. It is rather an affirmation of God's consistency and orderliness.

One must not deny that God has worked in miraculous ways at those times in history when He brought new revelation to man. Such the Scriptures affirm. When God broke into the world with revelation in the spiritual realm, He also broke into the world with miracles in the physical realm. New revelation and miracles go together. It was true with Moses. It was true with the prophets. It was true with Jesus. It was true with the apostles. Miracles confirmed revelation. If there is no new revelation, there is no need of miracles.

One must not deny the activity of God in the world today. He is still working. The nature of His work is orderly, constant and according to His laws of creation. Such is the nature of God. Such is compatible with God's "once for all" revelation in the Scriptures and His "once for all" confirmation of that Scripture by miracles. Such fits the observations of man and is a basic presupposition of the scientific method. God is a God of order.

ENDNOTES

[1]Matthew 28:20

[2]Ephesians 1:11

[3]Ephesians 3:16-20

[4]Hebrews 1:3

[5]Romans 1:21-22

[6]Luke 12:19

[7]Romans 11:22

[8]Romans 11:33-34

[9]Hebrews 1:2-3

[10]Colossians 1:15-17

[11]I John 5:14 see also I John 3:22

[12]Matthew 7:7-11

[13]Matthew 26:39; I John 5:14

[14]James 4:13-15

[15]James 4:2

[16]Matthew 7:7-11

[17]Acts 24:2 and Romans 13:14

[18]J. D. Thomas, "The Uses of Supernatural Power," Firm Foundation, (February 13, 1973) p. 103

[19]Daniel 4:25

[20]Romans 13:1

[21]John 19:11

[22]Esther 4:14

[23]Genesis 45:5,8

[24]Romans 9:17

[25]Philemon 15-16

[26]Hebrews 13:6

[27]I Corinthians 10:13

[28]Romans 8:28, 31-32

[29]Matthew 6:31-33

[30]Philippians 2:12

[31]Philippians 3:13

[32]Ephesians 3:20

[33]Genesis 1:2

CHAPTER 10

CONFUSION OVER CONTEMPORARY CLAIMS

Defining the Terms

Much of the confusion over contemporary claims of the miraculous can be resolved by defining the terms.[1]

The normal happenings of nature, no matter how wondrous, cannot be defined as miraculous in the New Testament sense. A majestic view in the mountains, a feeling of euphoria from a human experience, and the awesomeness of the birth of a child are all wondrous, but not miracles.

The unexplainable happenings of everyday life, no matter how mysterious, cannot be called miracles in the New Testament sense. They may be inconsistent with what one knows about the universe. They might be paranormal, but not miraculous. A hypnotic trance, participating in the mystery of ouija boards or experiencing the ecstatic utterances of automatic speech cannot be totally understood in the light of present knowledge. Such, however, cannot be called miracles in the New Testament sense. All of these phenomena are to be found within the human experience and are consistent with physical and psychological laws as they are known. They might be mysterious, yes, but miracles, no.

The unexpected and the odd happenings that are observed in the course of life, no matter how rare or uncommon, cannot be called miracles in the New Testament sense. The odds for such an event happening in the way it did, are staggering in magnitude. The event may be so rare that no one living has seen the like of it before. It is not miraculous in the New Testament sense unless it is inconsistent with the laws of creation. The birth of a two headed calf, a narrow escape from a burning house or winning a lottery with a ticket you found on a street might be odd and out of the ordinary, but they are not miraculous in the New Testament sense.

The unexplainable and unpredictable recovery from illness does not necessarily mean a miracle. Such happens among believers and non-believers, among both good and bad people and among the penitent and the reprobate. Such an event might happen simultaneously with prayer. Such an event might mystify the doctors. It might occur following a renewal of spiritual commitment. All of this does not mean a miracle has taken place. A person who has been diagnosed as having cancer might be healed. The rapid and complete cure of stomach ulcers might take place. There might be remission of a severe case of arthritis. All of these remarkable cures might not be understood, but that does not mean they are miraculous. Ignorance of how God works in healing the human body cannot be a reason to call a cure miraculous.

An event is a miracle in the New Testament sense only if it is instantaneous, complete and inconsistent with the known laws of medical science.

Miraculous claims which come in the context of emotional excitement and expectancy of a healing campaign do not fit the New Testament pattern. They might seem real at the time. A euphoria might accompany the event, and it might be interpreted as being from God. The symptoms of the illness might be temporarily relieved due to the adrenalin released in the body, but still this would not be identified with New Testament miracles. The anxiety one might have over some suspected illness might be relieved permanently because the symptoms were psychosomatic in their origin. This must not be mistaken for a real miracle of the New Testament. Such experiences as these are to be found in pagan religions both ancient and modern and must not be confused with the miracles of the New Testament.

There are very few of the claims of the miraculous which do not fit into one of the above categories. They fall far short of the pattern of New Testament miracles and can be explained in the same way that pagan wonders are understood. Most of the confusion over miraculous claims could be resolved by precise definition of terms and a clear understanding of the nature of the miracles of the New Testament.

Some Explanations for the Claims

Certainly one cannot ignore the miraculous claims coming from so many quarters. The people who believe they have experienced them are very confident. There are often marked changes in the person's lifestyle and personality when he believes he has experienced a miracle. God is praised and multitudes rejoice when the miracle story is told. Surely something must have happened to bring about all of this. How can such as this be explained if a miracle did not happen?

First, there is usually a misunderstanding of the breadth and suffi- ciency of God's natural laws.

Many happenings in the world are paranormal.[2] They do not con- tradict any of the known laws of the universe, but neither are they in the realm of the explainable normal.

Just as there are unexplainable cures that happen outside of the religious context which baffle the doctors, there are unexplainable cures which happen within the religious context. The latter are called miracles, not because they are different from the former, but because they are so interpreted by those who seek such. With the advance of medical science many of these paranormal cures are being better understood. When understood, they are rare and maybe odd, but still they are normal.

Much of the illness in the world may be classed as psychoso- matic. This means that there is no direct physical ailment, but the psyche (mind) is convinced that there is. The symptoms that are produced in the body are the same as if the illness were physical. Estimates vary among authorities, but it would be safe to say that between sixty and ninety percent of all illnesses are of this nature.

If a healer can convince a person he is well, his psychosomatic symptoms will disappear. He then will believe that he has been cured by Divine intervention. This accounts for some cures which are called mirac- ulous. This kind of healing is not a miracle, but it is real.

The human body is a marvelous creation which has been designed to meet emergencies. With proper stimulation, the brain can shut out pain. With proper stimulation, the adrenalin gland secretes fluids which cause the heart to quicken, the face to flush and the muscles to have greater strength. In times of fear, excitement and ecstasy the body will perform feats which are believed to be beyond its normal capacity. This phenomena can be observed in healing services. A person believes himself to be healed in the excitement of the highly emotional healing ceremony. He is able to do remarkable things. Later, however, the illness is still found to be present. This kind of healing is not a miracle, but it appears to be real at the moment of excitement.

The power of the mind over the body is remarkable. Even Plato made this observation.

> *Let no one . . . persuade you to cure the head, until he has first given you his soul to be cured by the charm. For this . . . is the great error of our day in the treatment of the human body, that physicians separate the soul from the body.[3]*

The suggestions of the physician or the healer to the patient can have a marked influence upon the cure of the ailment. Such suggestions alter the thinking of the patient, and this helps the healing process of the body.

Kelsey wrote of this.

> *Suggestion does have healing power. However, suggestion seldom cures the more seriously neurotic or psychotic patient; instead its success lies often in merely suggesting away the symptom, leaving the underlying cause to pop up again in some other, often more serious guise. Nor is it possible to tell exactly how suggestion or hypnosis works.[4]*

Cures from suggestions can take place both in the doctor's office or the healing campaign. It is not miraculous, but it is real.

Moral and ethical harmony can certainly affect one's health. The God who established the laws which govern the health of the body is the same God that reveals the moral and ethical teachings of the Scriptures. The moral laws of the Scriptures and the physical laws which govern the body are in harmony. One affects the other.

S. I. McMillen in his book *None of These Diseases[5]* demonstrates this principle from his own case studies as a medical doctor. The thesis of the book is a quotation from Exodus.

> *If you will give earnest heed to the voice of the Lord your*
> *God, and do what is right in His sight, and give ear to His*
> *commandments, and keep all His statutes, I will put none*
> *of the diseases on you which I have put on the Egyptians;*
> *for I, the Lord, am your healer.*[6]

The moral laws and the purification rituals of the Old Testament, McMillen suggests, were not only commands of God but also good health habits. The case histories contained in the book show that when a person alters his attitude and/or life style to conform to the teachings of the Scriptures, it can also be good for his health. This accounts for some of the success of what is now called "Holistic Medicine". This kind of healing can certainly take place in the context of the so called "divine healing" phenomenon. It is not miraculous, but it is real.

There should be no objections to any means that men use to heal the sick or make people live more in harmony with the law which God has given for human health. Every person should rejoice when those who are hurting are made to feel better.

The "divine healing" phenomenon goes beyond this. The methods listed above are good when seen as using what God has given in His creation to help people feel better. They are bad when interpreted as special favors God gives to certain people in response to certain ritual without Scriptural authority. They are bad in that they are attributed to special divine intervention contrary to the consistency and orderliness of God's natural laws. They are bad when they are used to manipulate people who are ignorant of what is happening in order to exalt a "healer" or obtain contributions under false pretenses.

Second, one can understand the so called "divine healing" phenomenon fully only when it is seen as a false religion. It has already been shown that when the New Testament speaks of signs in the latter times after the day of Pentecost, it refers to false prophets and lying wonders.[7]

This 'divine healing" phenomenon is a false religion because it has false doctrine associated with it. One of the points Moses gave to test a prophet was whether or not he conformed to the teachings given by God.

> *If a prophet or a dreamer of dreams arise among you and*
> *gives you a sign or a wonder, and the sign or the wonder*

> *comes true, concerning which he spoke to you, saying,*
> *let us go after other gods (whom you have not known) and*
> *let us serve them, you shall not listen to the words of*
> *that prophet or that dreamer of dreams; for the Lord your*
> *God is testing you to find out if you love the Lord your*
> *God with all your heart and with all your soul.*[8]

Jesus warned that false Christs and false prophets would arise with signs and use them as a means to lead people astray from the truth.

> *For false Christs and false prophets will arise and will*
> *show great signs and wonders, so as to mislead, if possible,*
> *even the elect.*[9]

Religious teachers who claim to have knowledge beyond the Scriptures are not to be followed, even if they seek to validate their claims by signs. False teaching is associated with the working of signs and wonders in the apocalyptic literature of Revelation.[10]

A prominent aspect of all eleven references in the epistles and Revelation to those who worked false signs was the false teaching connected with the signs.[11]

Without going into details about the falseness of the doctrines of religious leaders who claim miracles, one can observe some things which they all have in common.

There is an exaltation of the miracle worker. He is seen as a special messenger of God possessing great power. Such follows the pattern of another false wonder-worker in the New Testament.

> *Now there was a certain man named Simon, who formerly*
> *was practicing magic in the city, and astonishing the people of*
> *Samaria, claiming to be someone great; and they all, from the*
> *smallest to the greatest, were giving attention to him, saying,*
> *This man is what is called the Great Power of God.*[12]

It is significant that the word translated "power" is *dunamis* which is one of the words translated "miracle" in the New Testament. Simon claimed to be someone great and people thought him to be the great miracle man of God. The apostles worked real miracles, but they refused to be exalted. If the people tried to exalt them after they worked a miracle, they

refused to be thus honored. At Lystra, the people were seeking to worship Paul and Barnabas after they had healed a lame man. Paul
responded thus:

> *Men, why are you doing these things? We are also men of*
> *the same nature as you, and preach the gospel to you in order*
> *that you should turn from these vain things to a living*
> *God.*[13]

A second thing common to most who claim miraculous powers is that
they also claim inspiration. Sometimes this claim is for no more than a
still small voice directing the claimant's activities. Sometimes it is power
to know the needs of people and foreknowledge of events. Sometimes it
is bold prophecy concerning the end time and how God has revealed to
him the destiny of nations. Sometimes it is a claim for wisdom to discern
the signs and symbols of the apocalyptic writings of the Scriptures.
Sometimes it is a claim of having new revelation to add to the Scriptures
like the Book of Mormon or the writings of Mary Baker Eddy. In every
case, there is a claim of some kind of supernatural inspiration to know the
mind of God.

To claim such inspiration is to reject the sufficiency of God's revelation in the Scriptures. Such claims of new revelation make the New
Testament inadequate and incomplete. It makes the "New" Testament -
- - an "Old" Testament. The new revelation is the new New Testament.

The New Testament itself warns against accepting such new revelation. John pronounces judgment against those who would add or take
away "from the words of the book of this prophecy".[14] Paul warns
against those who would preach another gospel "contrary to" or "more
than " that which the Galatians had received. Such were "accursed" even
if they claim to be an angel from heaven. In refuting the claims of ancient
Gnosticism, which claimed more revelation than that revealed in the Scriptures, John tells the church not to receive any person who "goes too far
and does not abide in the teaching of Christ".[15] Jude affirms that the faith
was "once and for all delivered" to the saints.[16]

A third thing common to most who claim contemporary miracles
is that they seek money from those who hear them. Like Balaam of old,
they love the wages of unrighteousness.[17] Motivated by greed, such men
exploit with false words.[18] By playing on the needs of desperate people

and offering false hope, they manipulate their followers to fill their coffers with wealth. By emotional appeals and exaggerated needs, they beg their followers to sacrificially give money beyond their means. Such men who obtain wealth by such unethical means show the same lack of ethical concern in its use. In recent years a number of the popular "miracle workers" have found themselves in trouble with the IRS because of their dishonesty and their irresponsible use of funds. They beg from the poor to live like the rich in the name of religion. Like those that Paul warned about in his letter to Titus, they deceive "for the sake of sordid gain ".[19]

One cannot separate miracles from new revelation. Revelation is a message revealed from God. A miracle is the method by which God confirms such a message as being true. To speak revelation without miracles is inconsistent with the way that God has dealt with man in history.

To work miracles without some new revelation to confirm is inconsistent with the way miracles are used in Scripture. Trench makes this observation concerning the relationship of the words and works of Jesus.

> . . . *the true relation is one of mutual interdependence, the miracles proving the doctrines, and the doctrines approving the miracles.*[20]

It is significant to note that similar miracles are worked by contradictory religions. Each of the religions claims that "its" miracles confirm the validity of its message. The Roman Catholics have their Fatima and their weeping pictures. The Protestants have their claims coming from the Anabaptists, the Pentecostals and the Charismatics. Similar claims are associated with the beginnings of Mormonism, Christian Science and the Seventh Day Adventists. A multitude of other religious leaders have arisen claiming the miraculous and teaching totally different and contradictory doctrines. How can this be?

Perhaps one is true and the rest are counterfeits. This position is taken by many. Such can hardly be true since the nature of the different claims are similar to one another and different from the miraculous recorded in the New Testament.

Perhaps God has just revealed himself to different people in different ways. The doctrines are different, but the faith is a common one in a deeper sense than formal external teachings. Such an attitude is found in the contemporary charismatic movement. In it individuals of quite diverse doctrinal beliefs and radically different rituals unite in common fellowship. The thing that binds them together is the ecstatic utterances which they all experience and which they all understand as a miracle.

Perhaps neither of these explanations is true. Rather, the miraculous claims are not only like other "Christian" religions, but they are also like ancient pagan religions. They are false. Individuals from all world religions - - - ancient and modern, pagan and "Christian" and rational and irrational - - -all claim the same kinds of things. It makes little difference whether or not they believe in the God of the Bible or the inspiration of the Scriptures.

If the contemporary claims of the miraculous are false, how can they be explained? The following three things can help to understand these happenings.

First, a natural, explainable, human phenomenon is interpreted as miraculous. It might be a rare happening. It might be different from past experiences. It might even be paranormal. It is not contrary to the laws of nature as man knows them and therefore can not be classed as a miracle. It "becomes a miracle" only in the eyes of the beholder because he has so interpreted it.

Second, trickery has been used to deceive the uninformed. The ancient pagans would build their altars so one could conceal himself in a tunnel. When the worshipper would seek the answer of the gods, the one concealed would respond from his hiding place. The worshipper would interpret it as the voice of the gods and the priests would profit from their trickery. Religious healers still practice deceit. Many cases have been documented of accomplices planted in the lines of people coming for "healing". Electronic devices have been used to secretly give the healer information which he claimed was coming from God.

Third, testimony has been believed from those who have been deceived in one of the two ways listed above. Emotional, subjective testimony of an interpretation of an event in the past often falls short of the actual facts. Experience alone is not the criterion of a thing being true or false. Experiences sometimes contradict other experiences in one's own life or the life of others. One can believe a lie. Paul writes this very thing when warning against false sign workers.

> . . .*the one whose coming is in accord with the activity of Satan, with all power and signs and false wonders, and with all the deception of wickedness for those who perish, because they did not receive the love of the truth so as to be saved. And for this reason God will send upon them a deluding influence so that they might believe what is false, in order that they all may be judged who did not believe the truth, but took pleasure in wickedness.*[21]

One can only understand the so called "miracle working" phenomena when he comes to perceive the signs as being false. The passage just referred to speaks of "false wonders", "deception of wickedness" and "deluding influence". God allowed such false signs from false prophets as a part of His judgment upon those who reject the truth. He still does. Such accounts for some of the contemporary miraculous claims.

In the eleven passages which refer to miracle workers in the epistles, the words "false", "deceit", "defraud" and similar words are used to refer to signs. What has been promised has been fulfilled. Miracle workers use false and deceitful signs.

Some people are professional "healees". They are employed to be healed. They act out their part sometimes for money and sometimes for glory. These people are the "plants" in the healing campaigns to help stimulate the excitement and expectancy necessary to get others in the "mood" to be healed. Nothing is more dishonest or hypocritical than for such to be done in the name of Jesus.

Some healers are able, by their own strong personality, to gain control of the emotions of a desperate person and command his psycosomatic illness away. The cure is real, but it is not miraculous. The same can be done by a psychologist, a witch doctor or a skilled medical doctor. This healing is false - - - not in the sense that it is not real - - - but in the sense that it is claimed to be a miracle.

Some healings are false because they just do not happen. The person who claims to be healed is still sick. He has desired healing with such intensity and directed his thinking to that end so much that he believes himself healed. This is in spite of the fact that he still needs insulin for his diabetes, he still needs medication for his infection, he still needs a brace on his back and crutches for his legs. One can only pity the plight of such a poor deluded soul. Pity is not the word to use for the "faith healer" who has manipulated his mind into such a delusion. He is to be identified with the father of all deceit, the devil.

Questioning the validity of miraculous claims is a sensative matter. One is emotionally involved in what he believes to be true. For such to be questioned can be uncomfortable. If, however, what one believes to be true cannot be supported by the facts of the case, it should be exposed. In examining the claims of contemporary miracles, one must not be blinded by subjective emotionalism.

Just because miracles are claimed by a popular religious leader who say a lot of good things about Jesus and morality, does not make these claims true. Just because miraculous claims are believed by good and sensitive people does not make these claims valid. Just because the claims are made in the name of Jesus does not make them genuine. Jesus Himself said that people would claim to work wonders in His name, but that He did not know them.[22]

Contemporary claims of the miraculous are false because the evidence does not support the claim. There is no valid evidence for men walking on water, raising the dead, drinking poison without harm or healing a severed ear. All that it would take to show that a miracle is real would be to present objective evidence to prove it.

Those who saw the miracles of Jesus sometimes accused Him of using the power of Beelzebul, but they could not deny the validity of the miracle. Not only did His followers acknowledge His miracles as genuine, but so also did His enemies.[23] Those who saw the miracles of the apostles could not deny them even though they opposed their teachings. The evidence was real and could not be denied.

And seeing the man who had been healed standing with them, they had nothing to say in reply . . .What shall we do with these men? For the fact that a noteworthy miracle has taken place through them is apparent to all who live in Jerusalem, and we cannot deny it.[24]

Testimonies

One can only understand the "miracle working" phenomenon when he sees that the movement is based upon subjective testimony.

An interesting study could be made of this point alone. What is the kernel of truth or the seed of deceit which lies behind the testimony? What culture and communication patterns were involved in the development of the testimony? What variations are there in the testimony which are influenced by the environment? What psychological fulfillment is to be found in repeating the testimony? What part does testimony play in the expectancy of the religious community? A study of these questions would say little about the validity of the miracle, but they would say much about the personal needs of the one who claims a miracle.

Two things make the discussion of "testimonies" difficult.

First, testimonies are personal, subjective and tied up with strong religious feelings. To question their validity is to threaten both the ego of the testifier and the integrity of his person. In spite of this, one must ask for a "proof of claim". It is not enough to say, "the Lord spoke to me..." or this happened to me as a "miracle from God". How can one know if the happening is from God, the devil or from within his own psyche? John warns Christians to beware of such a naive faith.

> *Beloved, do not believe every spirit, but test the spirits*
> *to see whether they are from God; because many false*
> *prophets have gone out into the world.*[25]

There are unholy spirits as well as the Holy Spirit. There are false prophets as well as true prophets.[26] How can one know if a thing is a delusion from the devil, a humanistic hunch or a message from God? To say that one knows it by the way he feels is to retreat into the subjective. Saul felt that he was religiously right when he was wrong. He persecuted Christians in good conscience, feeling it was the thing to do.[27] Ignorance and unbelief had allowed his mind to be deceived.

If one's religious commitment and affiliation is confirmed by one's testimony, it makes it even more difficult to question the validity of the testimony. Not only must one recognize the possibility that such testimony might be wrong, but he must also recognize that his religious commitment and affiliation could be destroyed if it is. It indeed takes a strong faith in God and a strong desire for truth to test one's personal subjective testimony in the light of the Scriptures and reason.

Second, many testimonies are handed down or handed over from others much like the pattern of oral traditions. There are exaggerations which come from repetition. There is confusion with other testimonies. There are adjustments that are made to meet the needs of the hour. As a result of these factors, it is difficult to get back to the original facts.

Too often when one seeks to support the claims of the miraculous, it is done with testimonies he has heard from unknown people in far off places without documented records. He feels it is true because it has been repeated to him by someone he trusts. The story may be interesting to listen to, but it cannot carry much objective validity due to the transmission flaws in oral testimony. An illustration of this principle can be observed in watching the way gossip becomes clouded more and more as it is repeated. By the time a story passes through one hundred people, one can hardly know what to believe.

Summary

One must not conclude that the rejection of contemporary claims in any way invalidates belief in the New Testament miracles. They are two different things. The New Testament miracles are God's confirmation of men and their message. They are events contrary to the natural order of things in nature. Contemporary claims of the miraculous are nothing more than natural human phenomena which have been interpreted by men through ignorance and deception as coming from God. This can be demonstrated by a comparison of the two kinds of events.

Subjects: The New Testament healings were done on well known people who had observable sickness. They were performed with or without the faith of the one being healed. Such is not the case of contemporary claims.

Time for Cure: The New Testament healings happened instantly and without the preparation and screening of those seeking to be healed. Such is not the case of contemporary claims.[28]

Quality of Cure: The New Testament healings were complete. There were no failures or partial cures. Everyone was healed. There were no relapses. There was no merely "getting better". Such cannot be said of contemporary claims.[29]

Nature of illness: The New Testament healings included healing a man who had been lame for forty years, restoring the sight to one born blind, raising the dead, restoring several members of the body. The nature of the illness was objective, observable and undeniably real. Such cannot be said for contemporary claims.

Miracle Worker: The New Testament healings were done by men whose lives and messages conformed to the will of God. They sought no glory and accepted no money. Such cannot be said of those who make contemporary claims.

Purpose: The New Testament healings have as their purpose bearing witness to the men who worked them as being approved of God and their message as being truth. Such cannot be said of those who make contemporary claims.

Trench, in comparing the New Testament miracles with the miracles recorded in the apocryphal gospels, makes some incisive observations which fit the comparisons of the New Testament miracles with contemporary claims.

> *In nothing, perhaps, are these apocryphal gospels more worthy of note, than in the difference between the main features of their miracles and of those of the Canonical Gospels. . . . . . (miracles in the apocryphal gospels jj) . . .are never signs, but at the best wonders and portents. Every higher purpose and aim is absent from them altogether. It is never felt that the writer is writing out of any higher motive than to excite and feed a childish love of the marvelous.[30]*

Comparisons of the New Testament miracles with pagan wonders, pious fantasies or contemporary claims reveal the distinctive and unique qualities of the former. They are real. They are genuine. They have purpose.

ENDNOTES

[1]See pages 1-5; 10-11

[2]See pages 5-6

[3]Morton T. Kelsey, *Healing and Christianity*
(New York: Harper and Row, 1976) p. 46

[4]Kelsey, op. cit., pp. 83-84

[5]S. I. McMillen, *None of These Diseases* (Westwood, New Jersey:
Fleming H. Revell Company, 1968)

[6]Exodus 15:26

[7]See pages 70-72

[8]Deuteronomy 13:1-3

[9]Matthew 24:24

[10]Revelation 13:13; 16:13; 19:19-20

[11]See pages 56-59

[12]Acts 8:9-10

[13]Acts 14:15

[14]Revelation 22:18-19

[15]II John 9-11

[16]Jude 3

[17]II Peter 2:15

[18]II Peter 2:3

[19]Titus 1:10-11

[20]Richard Chenevix Trench, *Notes on the Miracles of Our Lord*
(Grand Rapids: Baker Book House, 1981) p. 60

[21]II Thessalonians 2:9-12

[22]Matthew 7:21

[23]John 9:47

[24]Acts 4:14-16

[25]I John 4:1

[26]Jeremiah 28:9

[27] Acts 23:1

[28] The one exception to this is in Mark 8:23-30

[29] The one exception to this is in Mark 8:14-29

[30] Trench, op. cit., pp. 27-28

CHAPTER 11

REJECTION OF CONTEMPORARY CLAIMS

It is not sufficient to show the marked differences between the genuine and the counterfeit. One must also show "how" and "why" the contemporary claims of the miraculous must be rejected.

No Evidence

Contemporary miraculous claims must be rejected because there is no objective evidence that they do occur.

One must not be confused by identifying the wondrous events of nature with a miracle. One must not be deceived by supposing that the odd, the rare or the paranormal is a miracle. One must not be taken in by psychic phenomena, clever tricks or pious frauds and identify such as a miracle. One must not be so gullible as to receive testimony of supposed events happening to unknown people in distant places and think that such are miracles. One must not be so full of expectation of Divine intervention that he will identify anything that he does not understand as an act of God.

If indeed a miracle occurs, where is the proof? One can investigate claim after claim after claim and all he ends up with is subjective material. There are personal subjective testimonies. There are hypothetical illnesses. There are emotional and ecstatic experiences. There are changes in feelings and life styles. There are interpretations that one makes that some natural phenomenon is a sign from God.

Where is the clear cut, objective evidence? Where are the undeniable facts which were evident in the New Testament miracles?

This kind of skepticism is not impiety. It is the same kind of critical thinking that the New Testament tells one to have when miraculous claims are made. There were false claims of miracles made in the New Testament times. They were tested and rejected.

Jesus warned His followers against false prophets and false Christs who would claim to work wonders. He told them to "believe them not".[1] John warned the Christians of his day not to believe those who made false claims about the Holy Spirit. They were to test the validity of the claims that were made.[2] Paul warned the Corinthians about false apostles and deceitful workers who disguised themselves as apostles of Christ. This should not seem odd since "even Satan disguises himself as an angel of light".[3] Jesus commends the church at Ephesus because they tried those who were false apostles.[4]

To ask hard questions of those who claimed miracles was the way that the New Testament Christians guarded against false teachers. The same process is valid today. The burden of proof rests on those who make the claim of miracles. Let genuine objective evidence be brought forth if their claim of miracles be true.

No Purpose

Contemporary miraculous claims must be rejected because there is no valid purpose which miracles serve at this time. It has already been shown that there are two purposes of the New Testament miracles. First there was the purpose to confirm the New Testament men and the New Testament message as being from God. Second, there was the purpose of showing that Jesus was the fulfillment of the Messianic prophecies of the Old Testament.[5]

Miracles would be needed again if there were a new Messiah. Miracles would be needed again if there were a new revelation from God. Since Jesus is the "once for all" sacrifice for sin, men do not need another Savior.[6] Since the faith which was delivered to the saints in the apostolic age was "once for all", there will never be a need for another faith to be given to men. Since the purposes of miracles have been accomplished,

there is no further need of them. There is not another Jesus who has
come that God must bear witness to through the miraculous. There has
not been a new revelation to man which must be confirmed by miracles.
Claims of miracles are rejected because they have no valid purpose.

The Jews in Jesus time sought signs. They wanted Jesus to work
signs so that they might, like Israel under Moses, have bread from
heaven without working for it.[7] They wanted a sign to validate Jesus'
cleansing the temple.[8] They wanted another sign after they saw Jesus
cast a demon out of a blind and dumb demoniac.[9] His answer was plain
to those sign seekers. They sought miracles but rejected the purpose of
miracles as being that of confirming Jesus' authority.

> *An evil and adulterous generation craves for a sign; and
> yet no sign shall be given to it but the sign of Jonah the
> prophet.[10]*

The purpose of signs is not for curiosity, power or material gain. They
do not have even as their primary purpose the showing of compassion
from the one who works them. Their purpose is confirmation.

The New Testament miracles have already confirmed Jesus and
His message. Those who seek them for other purposes stand just as
much condemned as the unbelieving Jews.

The rich man in Hades wanted a miracle. He asked Father
Abraham for the resurrection of Lazarus in order that he could go back to
earth and warn his five brothers "lest they also come to this place of tor-
ment". Father Abraham replied, "They have Moses and the Prophets; let
them hear them". The rich man in Hades did not think the Scriptures
were sufficient in their warning. He continued to seek a miracle.

> *No, Father Abraham, but if someone goes to them from
> the dead, they will repent! But he said to him, If they
> do not listen to Moses and the Prophets, neither will
> they be persuaded if someone rises from the dead.[11]*

Miracles are not needed when there are clear Scriptures. To seek a miracle when God has already given revelation is to misunderstand
completely the purpose of the miraculous. It can be said both of the rich
man in Hades and those who seek new miracles today, "If one rejects the

plain teachings of the Scriptures, he would not be persuaded to repent even if he saw a multitude of miracles".

The purpose of miracles is not to test God to see if He will keep His promises. The purpose of miracles is not to help one get himself out of the predicament.

One of the temptations the devil gave to Jesus in the wilderness sounds very much like the reasoning of those who seek after miracles today. In the second temptation, according to Matthew, we have the following conversation between Jesus and the devil.

> *Then the devil took Him into the holy city; and he stood*
> *Him on the pinnacle of the temple, and said to Him, If You*
> *are the Son of God throw Yourself down; for it is written,*
> ***He will give His angels charge concerning you;***
> ***and on their hands they will bear you up, lest you***
> ***strike your foot against a stone.*** *Jesus said to him,*
> *On the other hand, it is written,* ***you shall not tempt the***
> ***Lord your God.***[12]

This was a temptation for Jesus to show His power. The devil challenged Him to prove that He was the Son of God by producing a miracle. The purpose of the miracle would not be for confirmation. Jesus knew who He was. So did the devil. The devil wanted Jesus to work a miracle to test the promise of God. He even quoted Scriptures from Psalms 91:11-12.

You can imagine the persuasion of the devil which is not recorded. Like tempters in the twentieth century, he could have said: "Don't you believe the promise of God?"; "Don't you trust God who has promised that His angels will bear you up?"; "Don't you desire to have all that God wants you to have?"; "Put God to the test to see if He will keep His promise!". Jesus refused to yield to such temptations and quoted Scripture Himself, "You shall not tempt the Lord your God!".

A basic part of the temptation was that the devil was seeking to pervert the purpose of miracles. He wanted Jesus to put God to the test and see if He would keep His promises. Jesus refused to tempt God by asking for a miracle. The same answer must be given by His followers when they are tempted to ask for a miracle.

No Qualified Miracle Worker

Contemporary miraculous claims must be rejected because there are no living persons who are qualified to work miracles.

In the New Testament several groups of individuals had miraculous powers.

Jesus, the twelve and the seventy worked miracles during Jesus' personal ministry.[13] The apostles were able to work signs. This was a confirmation of their apostolic office.[14] The twelve and the seventy were able to work signs because Jesus had given them authority to do so.

Those upon whom the apostles laid their hands possessed miraculous powers.[15] Two of the seven men upon whom the apostles laid their hands in Acts 6 were able to work miracles at a later time.[16] The twelve men Paul converted at Ephesus could miraculously speak in other languages and prophesy after Paul laid his hands on them.[17] Timothy received a grace gift from the laying on of Paul's hands.[18] Numerous individuals at Corinth had received miraculous powers. They possessed spiritual gifts to do many kinds of miraculous things.[19] No where do the Scriptures say that they received these powers through the laying on of the apostles' hands, but such could well have been the case. Paul had been at Corinth for more than a year and had plenty of time and opportunity to lay hands on the Christians there in order that they might work miracles. After he was there he wrote them that "you are not lacking in any gift".[20]

Cornelius and his household received miraculous power to speak in other languages and prophesy. This was much like that which happened on the day of Pentecost.[21] They, like the apostles, had received the baptism of the Holy Spirit.

The power to work miracles was not distributed in a chaotic manner. Jesus, the Son of God and His apostles were those most prominent in working miracles. After them came those who received the baptism of the Holy Spirit and those who had received the laying on of the apostles' hands.

There are no individuals in these categories who are living today. The result is that there are no miracles today.

No Authority

Contemporary miraculous claims must be rejected because there is no Scriptural authority to suggest that they were to continue beyond the apostolic age.

Some would suggest that Jesus promised that miracles would continue. To support this claim they would refer to the statement Jesus made after giving the great commission, "these signs shall accompany them that believe".[22]

It has already been shown that the text does not say, "these signs shall be worked by those who believe". The promise is rather, "these signs shall accompany them that believe". The statements are not the same. Signs can accompany the preaching of the gospel directly as was done in the lives of the apostles. Signs can also accompany the preaching of the gospel through the Scriptures which record the signs. The first can be illustrated by a commentary Mark makes on this promise of Jesus.

> *And they went out and preached everywhere, while the Lord worked with them, and confirmed the word by the signs that followed.*[23]

The word was confirmed by miracles worked through the apostles. The people could see and believe that the message was from God.

The second can be illustrated by the statement of the apostle John about miracles. At the conclusion of his gospel he shows that written records of miracles also confirm the work.

> *Many other signs therefore Jesus also performed in the presence of the disciples, which are not written in this book; but these have been written that you may believe Jesus is the Christ the Son of God.*[24]

The word was confirmed by miracles recorded through the apostles. The people could read and believe that the message was from God.[25]

Some have been deceived into thinking that if Jesus "is the same yesterday and today, yes and forever", then miracles must still happen.[26] It should be observed that there is nothing in the context of this passage in Hebrews which refers to the miraculous. The passage is teaching that Jesus is the same, not that He works in the world the same way in every

generation. Jesus does not die on the cross every day or in every generation. Jesus is not resurrected every day or in every generation. The
word of God is not revealed anew in every generation. Neither are the
miracles which confirm the word worked in every generation. Jesus is
the same in every generation, but there are things that Jesus did once and
for all time. Working miracles is one of these things.

The New Testament itself predicts the passing of the miraculous.
It has already been shown that there was a decrease in the miraculous
activities from the Gospels to Acts.[27] There is even a greater decline
from Acts to the Epistles.[28] There is even a decline from the early to the
later epistles. All of this reflects the passing of the miraculous in the apostolic age.

This does not mean that God has ceased His work in the world.
This does not imply that Jesus having gone to heaven is unconcerned
with His followers on the earth. This certainly does not suggest that the
Holy Spirit is not working in the midst of the church today. God is alive
and working in today's world. The Holy Spirit still dwells in every
Christian. Jesus still works in the lives of individual men and rules the
nations.

The question is not "whether God works in the world", but "how
God works in the world". To deny contemporary miraculous claims
does not in any way nullify one's faith in the present work of God. Such
is an affirmation that God is working in the world but according to His
will in revelation and creation. Miracles do not happen because such is
the evidence from Scriptures, from reason and from observation.

The Scriptures themselves show that the miraculous was to pass
away. One can not place an exact date on their passing. One can not
know for certainty when the last miracle was performed. He can only
believe the promise that they would cease. Paul speaks of this in writing
to the Corinthians who gloried in the miraculous element of their gifts.

> *Love never fails; but if there are gifts of prophecy, they will*
> *be done away; if there are tongues, they will cease; if*
> *there is knowledge, it will be done away. For we know in*
> *part, and we prophesy in part; but when the perfect comes,*
> *the partial will be done away.*[29]

This passage does not identify with clarity what the perfect is. It does state that the spiritual gifts will pass when the perfect comes. Neither does it state the time that they shall pass.[30] This passage does teach clearly that the spiritual gifts like prophesy, tongues and knowledge will "cease" or "pass away". They are temporary, inferior and passing away while love never fails. Those who seek after such miraculous signs today should understand that Paul predicted their passing.

Paul makes a similar statement to the church at Ephesus. In speaking of the gifts given by Jesus when He ascended on high, he identifies some of them with the apostles, prophets, evangelists and pastor-teachers. He then says that they are to be used . . .

> . . *for the equipping of the saints for the work of service,*
> *to the building up of the body of Christ; until we all attain*
> *to the unity of the faith, and of the knowledge of the Son of*
> *God, to a mature man, to the measure of the stature which*
> *belongs to the fullness of Christ.*[31]

A significant word in this passage is "until". These gifts which assisted those persons in position of leadership in the early church helped them equip the saints in the work of building up the body of Christ. Paul shows that such gifts would be only "until" the unity of the faith was obtained and the church reached maturity. One cannot place a date on when that was, but he can know that Paul understood that such a time was coming.

R. C. Trench writes of this problem of fixing the exact time of the passing of the miraculous.

> *Few points present greater difficulties than the attempt*
> *to fix accurately the moment when these miraculous powers*
> *were withdrawn from the Church. This is difficult, because*
> *it is difficult to say at what precise moment the Church*
> *was no longer in the act of becoming, but contemplated in*
> *the mind of God as actually being; when to the wisdom of*
> *God it appeared that He had adequately confirmed the word*
> *with signs following.*[32]

When, in the wisdom of God, the word that was revealed through Jesus and the apostles was adequately confirmed, the miracles themselves

138

ceased. In the creation of the heavens and earth, God did not continue to create after He had spoken His laws into existence and creation was accomplished. He allowed the seed to bring forth after its kind. The law had been established. His purpose had been accomplished.

In the revelation of the Gospel to the world, God did not continue to work miracles after His word had been confirmed. He allowed the word to do its regenerating work. The gospel had been established. His purpose had been accomplished.

The miraculous spiritual gifts were temporary. They had an end-time. What evidence is there to suggest that this end-time has not already come? No Scripture promises the continuation of the miraculous gifts. There is no evidence that such are still happening. There are no persons living who fit the New Testament pattern of miracle workers. There is no reason for such to continue to exist. Both faith and reason demand that the contemporary claims of miracles be rejected.

No Distinctiveness

Contemporary miraculous claims are not distinctive from the claims of ancient pagan religions or non-Christian religions of today. This has already been shown.[33] How can one claim the miracle which he has seen is from the God of the Bible when the same kind of phenomena happens in the Hindu and the Spiritualist religion? What is distinctive about his claims?

How is it, that even within the religions who claim to follow Christ, there is such diversity of doctrine among those who claim miracles? The Charismatic Movement is to be found in every Catholic and Protestant church known to this author. The Charismatics of each of these groups claim miracles, but the doctrine they believe and the rituals they practice are radically different from one another.

One group will be unitarian and another group will be trinitarian. One group will pray through the saints and another group will reject such a practice. One group sprinkles babies and another group immerses adults only. One group rejects verbal inspiration of the Scriptures and another group holds such to be of fundamental importance. How can this be?

If the miracles they claim are really from God, then why does not God reveal the right teachings and the correct religious practices to them? Miracles in the New Testament were to show God's approval of those who spoke the Gospel message and the truthfulness of the message they spoke. How can contemporary miracles be from God if those who make such claims have contradictory doctrines and practices?

If one would suggest that only the miracles connected with his faith are real and the rest are counterfeit, he runs into a practical problem. The ones he claims are real are the same kind of phenomenon and are supported by the same kind of unreliable subjective evidence as those he claims to be counterfeit. For one to be real and the other counterfeit, then they have to have something distinctively different in their nature. Such cannot be found.

When those who claim contemporary miracles are able to show their miracles are distinctive from the others in alien and erroneous religions, then they might merit serious investigation. Such has not been done and can not be done. They are the same kinds of things based on the same kinds of evidence to influence the same kinds of people.

ENDNOTES

[1]Matthew 24:24

[2]I John 4:1

[3]II Corinthians 11:13-14

[4]Revelation 2:2

[5]See pages 81-82

[6]Hebrews 7:27; 9:12, 26

[7]John 6:26, 30

[8]John 2:18

[9]Mattthew 12:38

[10]Matthew 12:39

[11]Luke 16:30-31

[12]Matthew 4:5-7

[13]Matthew 10:1; Luke 10:1-20

[14]II Corinthians 12:12

[15]Acts 8:18

[16]Acts 6:8; 8:6

[17]Acts 19:1-7

[18]II Timothy 1:6

[19]I Corinthians 12:7-11

[20]I Corinthians 1:7

[21]Acts 10:44-48; 11:15-18

[22]Mark 16:17

[23]Mark 16:20

[24]John 20:30-31

[25]For a fuller discussion see Jimmy Jividen, *Glossolalia* (Fort Worth: Star Bible Publications, 1971) pp. 89-98

[26]Hebrews 13:8

[27]See pages 19-20

[28]See pages 63-64

[29]I Corinthians 13:8-10

[30]For a fuller discussion see Jividen, *op. cit.*, pp 116-128

[31]Ephesians 4:12-13

[32]Richard Chenevix Trench, *Notes on the Miracles of Our Lord* (Grand Rapids: Baker Book House, 1981) pp. 33-34

[33]See pages 97-98

Miracles: From God or Man?

CHAPTER 12

THEOLOGICAL CONSIDERATIONS

Some of the greatest difficulties in accepting contemporary miraculous claims are the theological consequences. The acceptance of such claims as being true present serious theological problems about the sufficiency of the Scriptures, the uniqueness of Christianity among world religions and the very nature of God.

Much more is involved than whether or not one wants to believe them. It is not just a matter that one can pass over with indifference if he takes his faith seriously. It is more than a mere item of curiosity or a discussion to stimulate intellectual exercise. It is more than examining the validity of existential feelings. Whether or not one accepts the contemporary claims of the miraculous has far reaching consequences about all that is Christian. Few issues reveal a man's theological presuppositions more fully or more clearly than his views on both the New Testament miracles and the contemporary miraculous claims.

Much of the tension that exists in denominational circles can be attributed to changing theological presuppositions. The creeds which now govern most of Protestantism and Catholicism were formulated by men of the past whose theological presuppositions were much different from those within those religions today. The theological presuppositions of these groups have changed, for better or worse, but the creeds remain the same. Much of the tension within the lives of the persons claiming to be Christians today exists because their views on the miraculous are different from the tradition of which they are a part. They find themselves giving approval to teachings and practicing rituals which are in conflict with what they really believe.

It is hoped that this chapter will focus sufficiently on the theological consequences inherent in accepting or rejecting the contemporary miraculous claims. By doing this perhaps the issue will be studied more seriously and critically. Perhaps one will then be able to resolve the conflict he finds within his own faith.

Sufficiency of the Scriptures

The sufficiency of the Scriptures is called into question by accepting the contemporary miraculous claims. There is no logical way one can accept these claims without also acknowledging supplementary revelation and additions to the Scriptures.

The basic purpose of miracles in New Testament times was to confirm the word.[1] Miracles and new revelation go together. What allows one allows the other. When one is present, so is the other.

The Mormon movement was consistent in its theological development. Mormons claim the miraculous, and they claim new revelation. Their claim of miracles, in their own thinking, confirmed the validity of the Book of Mormon and their other "inspired" books. The miracles they claim and the new revelation they espouse stand or fall together.

Often those in the Charismatic movement have failed to realize that accepting miracles carries with it the acceptance of new revelation. If they understood that such acceptance would make their Bibles obsolete and inadequate, they would be more critical of the miraculous claims.

The very nature of many of the contemporary miraculous claims makes them new revelation. If God is thought to have spoken to an individual through a still small voice, a vision or a dream, the result is new revelation. By definition it is so. If God is thought to have given someone the gifts of prophesy, tongues or the interpretation of tongues, it is new revelation by definition. Consistency demands that such new revelation be regarded with the same authority as the Scriptures themselves.

Peter explains the process of revelation as being the Holy Spirit moving men to speak.

But know this first of all, that no prophecy of Scripture is

> *a matter of one's own interpretation, for no prophecy was*
> *ever made by an act of human will, but men moved by the*
> *Holy Spirit spoke from God.*[2]

If indeed men speak today as they are moved by the Holy Spirit, then
what they say should be added to the Bible. It becomes new revelation
from God. It makes the "New" Testament in the present Bible in reality
an "Old" Testament.

Most individuals who would be supportive of contemporary
miraculous claims are not willing to go this far. They have not
considered the logical consequences of their misguided faith. One cannot
escape these consequences, however, when such a faith is taken to its logical end.

The New Testament scholar knows that the Scriptures affirm their
own sufficiency. Such is particularly emphasized in Paul's writing to
Timothy.

> *. . .and that from childhood you have known the sacred*
> *writings which are able to give you the wisdom that*
> *leads to salvation through faith which is in Christ Jesus.*
> *All Scripture is inspired by God and profitable for teaching,*
> *for reproof, for correction, for training in righteousness;*
> *that the man of God may be adequate, equipped for every*
> *good work.*[3]

In this passage Paul is speaking primarily of the Old Testament Scriptures
which Timothy had studied from his youth. In verse sixteen, however,
he makes an axiomatic statement which shows the sufficiency of the
Scriptures. These Scriptures are able to make the man of God complete.
Nothing more is needed to reveal the will of God or direct man in his
quest for God.

God's will revealed in Jesus Christ was not "here a little, there a
little" or "partly at this time and partly at another time". Jude shows that
it was one time and for all time.

> *. . . I felt the necessity to write to you appealing that*
> *you contend earnestly for the faith which was once for all*
> *delivered to the saints. For certain persons have crept in*
> *unnoticed, those who were long beforehand marked out*

> *for this condemnation, ungodly persons who turn the grace*
> *of our God into licentiousness and deny our only Master and*
> *Lord, Jesus Christ.*[4]

The word translated "once for all" is *hapax* which means "once for all time, not to be repeated". It is the same word that is used for the "once for all" sacrifice of Jesus Christ.[5] Just as Jesus' sacrifice was for all time, so also is the faith delivered to the saints in the New Testament period for all time. One does not need a new revelation from God any more than he needs a new Savior to die on the cross.

A passage in the closing verses of the New Testament shows the sufficiency of the Scriptures and warns against adding to and taking away from them. It was primarily written concerning the book of Revelation, but it gives a warning which applies to all Scripture.

> *I testify to everyone who hears the words of the prophecy*
> *of this book: if anyone adds to them, God shall add to him*
> *the plagues which are written in this book; and if anyone*
> *takes away from the words of the book of this prophecy,*
> *God shall take away his part from the tree of life and from*
> *the holy city, which are written in this book.*[6]

Similar warnings are given in the Old Testament.[7] God will not tolerate men who presumptuously claim additions to His word or changes in His laws in nature.

The Uniqueness of Christianity

The uniqueness of Christianity among the different world religions is called in question by the acceptance of contemporary miraculous claims. Nearly every religion of the world, be it pagan or of "Christian" variety; be it ancient or modern in time; be it witchcraft, spiritualism or the occult; all make miraculous claims. The uniqueness of the New Testament miracles was not in the fact of the miraculous claims, but in the nature and purpose of the miracles themselves.[8] Such cannot be said of the contemporary claims to miracles. With them come all of the trappings of their pagan counterpart. With them come all of the perverted purposes of miracles as expressed in the history of world religions.

Pagan religions claim to hear the voice of the gods, so it is with those who make contemporary miraculous claims in the name of Jesus. Pagan religions claim that their ecstatic utterances done in the context of religious ritual are from their god. The same is true with those who make similar claims in the name of Jesus. Pagan religions claim to cast out demons and heal the sick. The same is true with those who make similar claims of exorcism and healings in the name of Jesus.

There is nothing unique about contemporary miraculous claims when they are compared to similar claims in world religions. The theological consequence of this is that there is little substance to a religion that is no different from the paganism which it imitates.

An interesting documentation of this is seen in a little book written by Raphael Gasson entitled, *The Challenging Counterfeit.* In this book, Gasson gives his testimony of how he had been a medium in Spiritualism and participated in all kinds of supernatural experiences like healings, prophesying and speaking in tongues. He was converted to the Charismatic movement and came to believe that what he had been doing as a Spiritualist was merely a counterfeit of the real thing. The real thing was what he experienced as a Charismatic in healing, prophesying and speaking in tongues. The odd thing about this transformation is that much of what he did as a Spiritualist was the same as what he did as a Charismatic. The difference was in his interpretation of the events. Several statements in the book show this.

> *It is very obvious that Satan is using an extremely subtle counterfeit to the precious gifts of the Spirit and this should cause the Christian to seek the power of this baptism of the Holy Ghost and not be satisfied until he receives it, with the initial evidence of the speaking in other tongues as the Spirit gives utterance. . . . . .*

> *It should grieve the heart of every Christian to realize that Satan is doing the very same good works which the Lord commissioned His disciples to do, while the Church with all the supernatural powers of God at its disposal is neglecting to aspire after the gifts.[9]*

The purpose of Gasson's book seems to be exposing the counterfeit miracles of Satan and setting forth the genuine miracles worked by the Charismatics. What the book really does is to show that they are both the same thing. The claims of one are as valid as the claims of the other.

One of the unique aspects of Christianity is the distinctive nature of the New Testament miracles. If they are nothing more than pagan wonders and contemporary counterfeits, then the total content of the Christian message is called in question. Instead of establishing the validity of the Christian system, contemporary claims of miracles are undermining its very basis. It is this preposterous claim of the miraculous which has become the stumbling block to faith in the mind of many thinking people.

Desire for the Miraculous

In a classical study concerning the development of the Greek culture, E. R. Dodds makes the following statement:

> *In a guilt-culture, the need for supernatural assurance,*
> *for an authority transcending man's appears to be over-*
> *whelmingly strong . . . without Delphi, Greek society*
> *could scarcely have endured the tensions to which it was*
> *subjected in the Archaic Age.*[10]

Ecstatic utterances and other experiential practices played an important part in both the native Greek religion and the mystery cults which were imported from the East. Dodds suggests that such irrational experiences were necessary as an escape from the tensions of the Greek culture. The expanding knowledge, the mingling of diverse cultures, the stress of war and other factors put such a strain on the culture that men retreated into the irrational. These irrational experiences were cathartic and purged the emotions from their tensions.

There was a great need for salvation and a sense of communion with a personal god in the ancient Greek psyche. The mystery cults began to grow, the healing shrines became popular and oracles were consulted. The personal psychological needs in the individual and the cultural vacuum in the community demanded supernatural assurance.

In times of great cultural stress, there is a retreat from reason and reality to the supernatural. Dodds observed it in the ancient Greeks.

Religious historians perhaps one day will document this as one of the factors which stimulated the rise of the Charismatic phenomenon in the United States in the third quarter of the twentieth century.

This description of the cultural need and how men seek to fill it says nothing concerning whether it is true or false, good or bad or Divine or human. That is another question.

Is seeking after the miraculous a good thing? Does one in the twentieth century need the confirmation that comes from miracles? Does God want to show His children miraculous signs to confirm His love and compassion for them? Apparently many would give a positive response to these questions. This response would come more from the personal need that is felt than for the physical or Scriptural evidence.

It has already been shown that God does not approve of sign seekers.[11] The five times Jesus was asked for a sign, He responded by speaking of the resurrection.[12] What greater sign could mankind have for God's approval of Jesus than His resurrection? If the resurrection is not sufficient, then no sign will be sufficient. One who accepts the resurrection of Jesus from the dead will not be seeking after lesser signs.

Jesus rebuked the devil because he tempted Him to work a miracle as a test of the promise of the Scripture.[13] The true believer does not need a sign to prove what God has promised in His word. His faith comes not from signs but from the word of God.[14]

Jesus rebuked the sign seekers who refused to acknowledge His power as being from God.[15] He called them an" evil and adulterous generation". He gave them no sign save the sign of the prophet Jonah.

Jesus refused to work signs which His brothers requested as a public relations technique. Signs were not a means of gaining the popular acceptance of the masses.[16]

Jesus rebuked James and John because they wanted Him to work a sign to satisfy their feeling of vengeance. A Samaritan village had refused to receive Jesus and His company and the sons of thunder wanted retaliation.[17] Jesus did not work miracles on a personal whim or in a needless use of power.

Jesus showed the folly of sign seeking to produce faith in the story of the rich man and Lazarus. When the rich man wanted to send Lazarus back from Abraham's bosom to warn his brothers, Father

Abraham made a significant statement about the those who think signs are more powerful than the Word.

> *If they do not listen to Moses and the Prophets, neither*
> *will they be persuaded if someone rises from the dead.[18]*

One who rejects the plain testimony of the Scriptures cannot be persuaded by a miracle. Miracles are not a short cut to faith. It is tempting God to seek after miracles when God has already given revelation. They were still taunting Jesus to perform signs even while He was upon the cross.

> *In the same way the chief priests, along with the scribes and*
> *elders, were mocking Him, and saying, He saved others;*
> *He cannot save Himself. He is the King of Israel; let Him*
> *now come down from the cross, and we shall believe in Him.[19]*

Just as the devil tempted Jesus to work a miracle for selfish benefit at the beginning of His ministry, so on the cross at the close of His ministry He was tempted the same way.[20] On both occasions the devil was trying to get Jesus to put God to the test. The devil quoted Scriptures and asked for a sign. Jesus response was "Thou shalt not tempt the Lord thy God". If one trusts God, he does not need to test Him by asking for a sign.

Those who were sign seekers in Jesus' day were rebuked. Sign seeking was pictured as being the desire of an evil and adulterous generation. They were guilty of the sin of testing God to see if He would keep His promises. They asked for a sign when they had already rejected the revelation of God in the Scriptures.

The same teaching applies to sign seekers today. If one desires a sign from God, the first question that needs to be asked is "Why?" Has not God revealed His will sufficiently in the Scriptures? Are not the signs recorded in the Scriptures of great enough number and magnitude to be sufficient? One's response to sign seekers today should be, "Thou shalt not tempt the Lord thy God!". One should quit desiring that which God does not give and man does not need.

Nature of God

The very nature of God is called in question by the acceptance of contemporary claims of miracles.

The Bible teaches that God is a God of order, not of chaos. In the beginning He created the *kosmos* out of chaos and saw that it was good.[21] He ordered nature so that it followed a plan and a consistent pattern. The ocean stays within its bounds. The planets remain in their orbits. The seed brings forth after its kind. The universe that God created is orderly.

God worked according to plan and pattern in unfolding His scheme of redemption. There were promises to the patriarchs. There were patterns in the tabneracle and the sacrifices in the temple. There was a plan predicted by the prophets. It all fit together because God is a God of order.

Miracles were in the plan of God. To show that some man or some message had His sanction, God would change His order. This called attention to the Divine approval of what was happening. After all, it was God who established the order, and it was only God who could intervene and change this order for His purposes.

These miracles were not done without purpose or without plan. Supernatural power was behind each one. This makes them different from the counterfeits of the devil, false religions and magicians.

If miracles were worked without plan or purpose in the world, then God would be a God of chaos. If God could be forced to do the will of man because He had been manipulated by some magic formula or past promise, then such a God would be too small. If God worked miracles at the bidding of man without regard to His established order in the universe or His plan in revelation, then He could not be trusted.

If God makes exceptions to His laws in nature in order to work a physical miracle, how can one trust His laws of revelation by which one receives salvation. If a seed does not produce after its kind in the physical realm, how can one be sure that the blood of Christ removes sin in the spiritual realm. The God who ordered creation is the God who gave revelation. If the laws of creation are not consistent, how can one trust the laws of revelation?

The very nature of God is wrapped up with the doctrine of miracles. To accept contemporary claims to miracles is to cast doubt on the orderliness and the consistency of the God of Creation and Revelation.

The Nature of Faith

Faith in Jesus Christ is based on the word of God and the testimony that it gives to the miracles of Jesus and the apostolic company.[22] The nature of faith is such that it cannot be proven by the scientific method or the logic of philosophy. It comes from a willing acceptance of the testimony given in the Scriptures.[23] Such a faith is not reasoned, but it is reasonable. One does not put his mind in neutral in order to believe. He does not disdain reason, logic and the empirical investigation of data. He has to use his mind to read Scripture, to discern the meaning of Scripture and test teachers to see if they are false.

It is at this point that those who believe contemporary claims to miracles come in conflict with those whose faith is based upon hearing the word of God. A statement from Mel Tari's book entitled, *Like a Mighty Wind* will demonstrate this point.

> *The main difference between science and Christianity*
> *is this: science we must experience to believe;*
> *Christianity we must believe to experience.*[24]

Right before this statement, Mel Tari admonished his readers to "take out that small computer which is your brain and put it in a little box and shoot it to the moon. Then let God use your heart". Making experience the basis of faith is a folly followed by multitudes in religion. Such a basis of faith will not endure the test of reason or survive the trials of time. To make experience the basis for faith is to undermine the very foundation of a Biblical faith. Experiences change with time. Experiences of one contradict the experiences of others and even one's own past experiences. They cannot be trusted. They are as fickle as the emotions of man.

Many who have their faith founded on what they have "experienced" in miraculous claims will lose their religious commitment as they begin to understand the falseness of such claims. Faith based upon fantasy will fade when truth is known. Faith based upon a misunderstanding of the paranormal will die when such is fully understood. Faith based upon a fraud will be shattered when the fraud is exposed. The only enduring faith is that which comes from the Word of God.

It is on this very point that the battle must be waged between those who accept and those who reject contemporary miraculous claims. It is at this point that one must come to grips with in his own quest for faith. Can truth be known from emotional experiences? Are feelings an adequate basis for faith? If one refuses to be abated in his own beliefs by objective evidence or reasoned arguments, how can his faith endure?

One cannot survive very long spiritually if, while living in a world of law, order and reason, he holds to an irrational faith. Truth is more than just what one perceives it to be. It is real, objective, reasonable and eternal. If this were not so, then God would be chaotic, the Scriptures would be full of error and Jesus Christ would only be a figment of man's own emotional fantasy.

ENDNOTES

[1] See pages 78-81

[2] II Peter 1:20-21

[3] II Timothy 3:15-17

[4] Jude 3-4

[5] Hebrews 7:27; 9:12, 26

[6] Revelation 22:18-19

[7] Deuteronomy 4:2; Proverbs 30:5-6

[8] See pages 97-98

[9] Raphael Gasson, *The Challenging Counterfeit* (Plainfield, New Jersey: Logos Books, 1972) pp. 90, 114

[10] E. R. Dodds, *The Greeks and the Irrational* (Boston: Beacon Press, 1957) p. 75

[11] See pages 29-30

[12] Matthew 12:38; 16:1; Luke 11:16; John 2:18; 6:30

[13]Matthew 4:5-7, see also pp. 134

[14]Romans 10:17

[15]Matthew 12:38, see also pp. 29-30

[16]John 7:3-4

[17]Luke 9:52-56

[18]Luke 16:31

[19]Matthew 27:41-42

[20]Matthew 4:1-11, see also pp. 134

[21]Genesis 1:1-31

[22]Romans 10:17; John 20:30-31

[23]John 7:17

[24]Mel Tari, *A Mighty Wind*
(Carol Stream, Illinois: Creation House, 1972) p. 61

CHAPTER 13

CONCLUSIONS

The New Testament miracles and the contemporary claims of the miraculous are not the same. They are different from one another in many ways. They are different in source. One is an act of God, and the other is either the deceit or misunderstanding of man. They are different in substance. One is contrary to the natural laws of the universe, and the other follows the consistent orderly pattern of the universe. They are different in purpose. One was used by God to confirm new revelation to man and the other is used to manipulate men and give power and wealth to the "miracle worker". They are different in effect. One was done immediately, completely and without failure while the other is done sometimes, partially , after emotional and psychological preparation of the persons involved and only in the perception of the believer. They are different in validity. One is true and cannot be denied by the witnesses, and the other is false and cannot be proven by its claimants.

How God Works

The basis for rejecting contemporary claims of miracles is not in any way questioning the power of God or His work in the world. The question is not "Does" God work but "How" God works. Does He work according to His will in creation and revelation, or is He chaotic and inconsistent. Does He uphold the order He made in creation and the law He revealed in revelation, or is He untrustworthy and not dependable in His relationship with men? If one believes that the later is true, then his view of God is too small.

The question is not whether God is able to work miracles. Certainly He is. He has done so and will do it again when Jesus comes. The question is, "Does God follow his own laws?". Does God limit Himself to the order He established in creation and the laws He gave in revelation? God is powerful enough to do whatever He wills. The nature of God is such, however, that He wills to work in an orderly way.

God is able to destroy the world with a flood, but will He? No, He will not. He has set the rainbow in the sky as a sign of His promise. He will not break that promise.

God is able to grow a watermelon out of an acorn, but will He? No, He decreed at creation that a seed would bring forth after its kind. He will not break the law He made.

God is able to save an impenitent liar, murderer and thief, but will He? No, He will not because He has established in the Scriptures the law of "repent or perish".[1] The loving, unmerited grace of God does not run contrary to His immutable will which He established at creation and which He revealed in Scripture. Because of this we can have assurance that God's promises are true and His judgments are sure.

One can trust God's laws. One can trust God's promises and warnings. One can trust the orderliness and consistency of His created universe. God is a God of order.

The question is not whether or not God heals. Certainly He does. No one is healed unless it is accomplished by God. The question is "how does He heal?". Does He heal according to the natural bodily processes or does He heal contrary to them?

Natural healing is a marvel. If one cuts his finger, the natural functions of the body begin the healing process immediately. The blood clots. White corpuscles begin to destroy bacteria. Red corpuscles begin to repair the injured cells. The laws which God decreed for the bodily functions begin the healing procedures. It is no less a work of God because it is natural.

The question is not whether or not the New Testament miracles are real. Certainly they are. One believes them --- every one of them - - - on the basis of the testimony of the inspired Scriptures. This faith is confirmed by the results they produced in the lives of the apostles and the very existence of the church. The New Testament miracles are unique. They are not like the pagan wonders of the past or the contemporary miraculous claims of the present.[2] They had as their purpose the confirmation of the men and the message associated with Jesus and His apostles. The question is not concerning New Testament miracles, but it is concerning contemporary claims of miracles. They are different.

The one is from God and the other is from man. The one is genuine and the other is a counterfeit. The one has confirmation as its goal, the other is without Divine purpose. The one could not be denied even by enemies; the other is clearly explainable through natural causes.

The question is not whether or not God answers prayer or works in providence. Certainly He does. The Scriptures promise that He did and will. History demonstrates that He did in the past, and faith assures one that He does in the present. The real question is "How does He do it?".

Does He do it in an orderly way following His laws of creation and revelation, or does He do it in a chaotic way without plan or consistency?

Paul understood that the working of the predestined plan of God is "according to the counsel of His will".[3] God's will and God's plan and God's laws do not contradict.

Is one to expect God to play havoc with either His order in creation or His laws of revelation when He answers the Christian's prayer? John said that Christians were not to pray for that which is contrary to God's will. Following the promise that "if we ask anything according to His will, He hears us", he said that one should not pray for one who sins a sin leading to death. This would be contrary to His immutable will.

> *If any one sees his brother committing a sin not leading to death, he shall ask and God will for him give life to those who commit sin not leading to death. There is a sin leading to death; I do not say that he should make request for this.*[4]

One of the conditions of prayer is that it be according to the will of God. Jesus taught His disciples to pray, "Thy will be done, on earth as it is in heaven".[5]

Even Jesus' prayer in the garden was "yet not as I will, but as Thou wilt".[6] Jesus did not ask God to go contrary to His eternal plan of redemption to accomplish something which would take away the suffering Jesus was about to endure.

It would be rather presumptuous to pray for something to happen which is contrary to either God's laws of creation or His will in revelation.

One would not want to pray for God to save an infidel in his unbelief. It would be contrary to His law of revelation - - - "he who has disbelieved shall be condemned".[7]

One would not want to pray for God to heal a person contrary to His laws of creation. God's will is to be done not only in the spiritual but also the physical realm. It would be a contradiction to pray, "Thy will be done" and then in the same prayer ask God to contradict His laws of nature in healing a person. Prayer is tuning our desires to God's will as much as it is seeking God's help in fulfilling our desires.

Listening with an Understanding Heart

The popularity of miracles in the contemporary culture is evidence that there are a great many people who need to be assured that God still works in the world. This cannot be ignored. If a question is not answered with truth, people will listen to a lie. If a need is not filled by that which is genuine, it will seek to be filled with that which is a counterfeit.

The great desire for miracles and the seeking after signs is a judgment upon the established religion of this age. Cold obsolete creeds, too often, have replaced Jesus as the focus of faith. Ecclesiastical machinery and non-biblical traditions have, too often, taken the wonder out of worship. Humanistic sociological concerns have, too often, crowded evangelistic zeal out of the work of the church. Popular psychological methodology has, too often, dulled the power of the life changing proclamation of the gospel. All of this could be called the "humanizing of the church". God is left out of religion and is relegated to a realm beyond man's day by day activities.

Those who seek to be the church of Jesus Christ as reflected in the Scriptures should take heed. In refuting the false prophets who work false signs, one must not fall under the temptation to ignore the real activity of God in the current events of man. God still lives and works in the world today and Christians should say so.

Nothing is gained when one sees error on the left, by fleeing into error on the right. The false claims of contemporary miracle workers can not be refuted by refusing to affirm that God still works in the world. The false teaching of the miraculous working of the Holy Spirit today cannot be corrected by teaching that the Holy Spirit works only through the Word of God. The false teaching of manipulating God through prayer demands and bargaining vows cannot be refuted by questioning the power of prayer. The false teaching that God will make one's decisions for him by "putting out a fleece" cannot be corrected by denying the need one has to seek God's direction in planning his goals. The false teaching that God will make one wealthy by giving cannot be refuted by denying His providential care.

The best way to expose the counterfeit is to reveal the genuine. The best way, and perhaps the only effective way, to expose experiential religion with its miraculous claims and exaggerated testimonies is to affirm the present work of God in the world. People satisfied with food will not be hungry for garbage. People who believe the truth will not be tempted to follow error. People who know God will not be flirting with the devil. People who believe that God works in their lives in an orderly way will not be deceived into believing that God works contrary to His laws of creation and revelation.

Summary

To understand the New Testament miracles, one must define what they were and how they were unique.

The words translated for the miraculous events in the New Testament reveal much about the nature of miracles. Focusing on their source, they were power --- power from God. Focusing on the response of those who saw them, they were wonders --- striking awe in their hearts. Focusing on the event itself, they were works --- something was happening in history. Focusing on their purpose, they were signs --- confirming that the man and message were from God.

The New Testament miracles were unique because, unlike the miracles performed by pagan wonder workers, they were above nature and not governed by the consistent observable laws God spoke into existence at creation.

To understand the contemporary claims of the miraculous, one must understand what they are and why they are not to be believed.

First, contemporary claims of miracles are false because they do not fit the pattern of New Testament miracles. They consist of tricks, frauds, paranormal happenings, psychosomatic cures and psychological phenomena. They can all be understood within the realm of human experiences and follow the laws that are observed in nature. They are common in all world religions --- ancient and modern, Christian and pagan --- and are sometimes found completely outside the religious context.

Second, contemporary miraculous claims must be rejected not only because they are false but also because of the theological consequences of accepting them. To accept such claims is to deny the sufficiency of theScriptures, is to compormise the uniqueness of Christianity among world religions and is to question the very nature of God.

The New Testament miracles were from God, but the contemporary claims of miracles are from man.

END NOTES

[1]Luke 13:3

[2]See pp. 127-128

[3]Ephesians 1:11

[4]I John 5:16

[5]Matthew 6:10

[6]Matthew 26:39, 42, 44

[7]Mark 16:16

SCRIPTURE INDEX

163

Printed in the United States
33726LVS00002B/223-246

9 780892 255443